BENNETT HOUSE
cookbook

Kentucky Delights

BENNETT HOUSE cookbook

Kentucky Delights

by

Rita Smart

Happy Cooking!
Rita

10-digit International Standard Book Number 0-9797835-0-X
13-digit International Standard Book Number 978-0-9797835-0-0
Library of Congress Card Catalog Number 2007936194

Cover design and book layout by Asher Graphics
Photos on pages 7, 21, 41, 44, 56, 67, 68, 75, 85, 96, 103 and 140 courtesy of John Gentry, Camera for Hire, Perryville, Kentucky.

Manufactured in the United States of America

All book order correspondence should be addressed to:

Bennett House Books
419 West Main Street
Richmond, Ky. 40475

859-623-7876

smart@bennetthousebb.com
www.bennetthousebb.com

introduction

Writing a cookbook presents problems and we solve them as we go along. My problem was getting my recipes in order and figuring out the cooking directions so readers could understand. The working of this book started with my work as a county extension agent for home economics (later called family and consumer sciences) at the University of Kentucky. This job introduced me to folks all across the state, especially central Kentucky. Over the years, I worked with Extension Homemaker Clubs and these members were among some of the best cooks in the country. I would always ask for their recipes and jot them down on a napkin, envelope or scrap paper. I was organized enough to put them in a certain kitchen drawer but never really got around to making neat, clean, concise cards or pages in an organized form. I knew how to cook and guess I just assumed everyone else did.

This book is dedicated to those friends, family members and great cooks who shared their love of cooking over the years. I am especially proud to have a neat, organized selection of my recipes to pass on to my two daughters, Angela Penn and Ashley Tabb. They are beyond my wildest dreams the most organized, efficient and beautiful women I could have ever imagined.

I was especially fortunate to have had a second career at the Bennett House. This provided me an opportunity to use all the recipes, lessons and tidbits I have acquired over the years. The Bed and Breakfast, as well as the monthly teas, provides an opportunity for guests, town-folks, friends and neighbors to share in this wonderful experience. Even though old-fashioned cooking and entertainment are almost a thing of the past, people still long for a short time to slow down, share conversation and partake of great food.

contents

bennett house history

The historic, old home located on Main Street, Richmond, Kentucky was known as the "Bennett Place." Mrs. Elizabeth Chenault Bennett purchased the lot in 1888 after the death of her husband, Samuel Bennett. She hired the prominent Cincinnati architect, Samuel E. desJardins, to draw plans for the Queen Ann style house touched with Romanesque detailing. Supervising the building of the house from 1889 to 1890 was Mrs. Bennett's son, James, whose wife Sarah (Sally) was the daughter of the notorious Cassius M. Clay and Mary Jane Warfield. Mr. Clay was minister to Russia during the Lincoln administration and his family often accompanied him on European trips.

Nay and Farry Coy bought the house in 1957. Mrs. Coy used it as her antique store, Westover Terrace, in the 60s and 70s. In May, 2000, Richard and Rita Smart purchased the business and expanded it, while protecting the integrity of the property.

Today the Bennett House represents not only a successful bed and breakfast but also a place of Richmond hospitality. Rita and Richard have combined their talents to provide a setting for local and out-of-town visitors to enjoy. The Smarts have made available their "architectural jewel" to the public for weddings, receptions, birthday galas, and bridal luncheons, plus their special "once-a-month English Tea Party."

Come and enjoy their southern hospitality on the first Saturday, every month, as Rita sets up tables covered with antique linens and fresh flowers for the season. She'll serve guests from her fine china and wow them with her incredible Kentucky Delights such as scones, lemon curd, little party sandwiches, cakes, savories and more. You're kindly invited...

Rita and Richard Smart

bennett house ladies

The Bennett House has been home for a number of outstanding ladies over the years. Belle Bennett moved into the home with her mother at the time the house was built. She later had an apartment at the Glyndon Hotel. Ms. Belle was instrumental in raising money to establish Scarritt Bible and Training School of Kansas City and Nashville as well Paine College in Augusta, George, a school for Negro girls. She established Sue Bennett Memorial College at London, Kentucky in 1892, in memory of her sister who also lived at the Bennett House.

Sarah Clay Bennett belonged to the "delicious modes of the 1860s – when crinolines and curls, bracelets and earrings were the fashion." She was driven through the streets of Washington, down Pennsylvania Avenue with President and Mrs. Lincoln. She saw, as a young women, the long line of chariots drawn up before the palace of the Czar of Russia at St. Petersburg – and swept up the great stairway to make her bow to the Czar and Czarina.

She returned home to be the belle of "White Hall" and to celebrate her wedding, a beautiful event. Then the "great cause of women" was called to her attention and she and her two sisters, Mary and Laura Clay were among the earliest to espouse the Cause of Equal Rights for Women and Women's Suffrage. She could just as easily have said "Let someone else do it, I have my family and the Bennett House to look after" but not so, — and like her father, Cassius M. Clay, who did not leave the cause of Abolition to others — she took up the battle of Equal Rights for all womankind.

In the 1880s she walked down the streets of Richmond with Susan B. Anthony who had come to lecture at the courthouse. She addressed the Suffrage Committee of the United States Senate in 1912 in Washington, D.C. on the subject of suffrage for women.

The victory was won with an amendment to the United States constitution, granting suffrage to women. As advocates of this great cause, Sarah Bennett and his sister, Laura Clay attained a national reputation.

through the years-

now & then

RITA PORTRAYING BELLE BENNETT

The Bennett House ladies live on! Belle Bennett was noted for her work for the Southern Methodist Episcopal church. She raised millions of dollars to educate pastors and missionaries. Her character is portrayed each fall in Richmond's Stroll Thru the Past.

Another Bennett lady, Sarah Clay Bennett, along with her sisters, Mary and Laura, were among the earliest to espouse the cause of Equal Rights. "Sally" is portrayed as the tour guide character each summer for the Richmond historic downtown walking tour.

Virginia Herndon's Cheese Loaf

Two 24-ounce containers cottage cheese, drained
8-ounce package cream cheese, softened
1 teaspoon salt
1/2 cup sugar
Two 1/4-ounce envelopes unflavored gelatin, soaked in 1/4 cup cold water
1/2 cup chopped nuts
2 tablespoons grated onion
1 red or green bell pepper, chopped
2 ounces stuffed olives, chopped

Cream the cottage cheese, cream cheese, salt and sugar in a mixing bowl using a fork or pastry blender. Quickly stir the soaked gelatin into the cheeses. Add the nuts, onions, peppers and olives, reserving 10 olives for garnish. Oil a 5-cup ring mold. Arrange the olive garnish in the bottom of the mold and press cheese firmly into it. Refrigerate overnight and remove from the mold. Serve with Cousin Melvina's Dressing.

Cousin Melvina's Dressing

1/2 cup sugar
1/4 cup vinegar
2 tablespoons finely chopped onion
1 teaspoon paprika
1 teaspoon salt
1 teaspoon dry mustard
1 teaspoon celery seeds
1 cup oil

Combine all the ingredients except the oil in a blender. Blend in the oil very slowly, almost drop by drop. The mixture will thicken by the time all the oil is added. Serve with Cheese Loaf.

The Herndon Family Farm is now the Battle of Richmond Civil War Park located on U.S. 461 south of Richmond. Virginia Herndon served this Cheese Loaf as a salad or side dish for many Extension Homemaker club meetings and church dinners. The cottage cheese was made on the farm so it was always available when company came.

Sweet Muffins

1/2 cup butter
1 cup sugar
2 eggs, well beaten
2/3 cup milk
1/4 teaspoon salt
2 cups all-purpose flour, sifted
3 teaspoons baking powder
1 teaspoon vanilla extract

Cream the butter in a mixing bowl. Add the sugar gradually; blend thoroughly. Add the eggs and mix. Sift the flour, salt and baking powder in a small bowl. Add to the butter mixture alternately with the milk. Add the vanilla. Bake in coated muffin tins at 375 degrees for 25 minutes.

Beaten Biscuits

7 cups all-purpose flour, sifted
2 teaspoons baking powder
4 tablespoons sugar
1 teaspoon salt
1 cup lard
2/3 cup milk
2/3 cup ice water

Combine the flour, baking powder, sugar and salt in a mixing bowl. Add the lard and work in thoroughly. Combine the milk and water in a small bowl and add slowly to the flour mixture, kneading until stiff dough forms. Divide the dough in half for ease of handling. Put the dough through beaten biscuit kneader or beat with a wooden rolling pin thoroughly. Combine the dough batches and repeat beating process at least 75 to 80 times. A velvety smooth dough about 1/4–inch thick is your goal. Cut with a 1-inch biscuit cutter. Place on a baking sheet and punch twice all the way through with a fork. Bake at 300 degrees for 35 minutes. Reduce the heat to 250 degrees for another 10 minutes or until the biscuits are slightly pink on top and bottom.

Makes 8 dozen.

Baked Country Ham

15 to 20-pound Kentucky country ham
1 cup vinegar
1 cup brown sugar
4 tablespoons pickling spice
1/2 cup brown sugar
2 to 3 tablespoons bread crumbs
1 teaspoon ground cloves
20-ounce can chunky pineapple, drained
Whole cloves

Soak the ham overnight in the vinegar and enough water to cover. Place the ham in a large roaster, fat side up, with clean water just to cover. Add 1 cup brown sugar and pickling spices. Cover and bake at 300 degrees for 4 hours. Remove from the oven and cool in the roaster. Debone and skin the ham. Combine 1/2 cup brown sugar, bread crumbs, ground cloves, pineapple and whole cloves and rub on the ham. Return to the oven and bake until brown. Cool thoroughly and thinly slice.

Makes 30 servings.

Through the years, recipes have been passed down from families and friends. I find there are basically no new recipes, only ones that have been adapted due to lack of ingredients, human mistakes or the desire to experiment. As with life, there is no one exact way to do everything. But use your own unique methods and individual techniques to create a culinary masterpiece. In the end, it usually turns out to be a "delight" especially if it tastes good.

Crème de Volaille

4 to 5-pound chicken
3/4 to 1 cup canned mushrooms, drained
2 tablespoons flour
2 tablespoons butter or margarine
1 cup milk or cream
1 tablespoon butter or margarine
3 eggs
Salt and pepper to taste
Parsley, chopped
Onion, grated

Boil the chicken until tender. Pick the meat from the bones and grind. Grind the mushrooms and combine with the chicken. Cook the flour, butter and milk (part cream lifts the flavor tremendously) in a saucepan, to make a cream sauce. Mix 1 cup of cream sauce to 3 cups chicken and mushroom mixture. Add the butter and eggs; beat well. Season with salt, pepper, parsley and onion. Pour into a coated mold and steam 1 1/2 hours. Serve with rich cream mushroom sauce.

I found this can also be cooked in a glass casserole dish with a lid. Set the dish in a pan of water while cooking.

Créme de Volaille was served at many family events and ladies club meetings. It was the early form of chicken casserole.

Kentucky Sauce for Ice Cream

1 cup brown sugar
1 cup white sugar
1 scant cup water
1 orange
1 lemon
1 cup strawberry preserves
1 1/2 cups chopped pecans or walnuts
1 cup Kentucky bourbon

Cook the brown sugar, white sugar and water in a heavy saucepan until it spins a thread. Remove from the stove. Add the strawberry preserves, nuts and bourbon to sugar mixture. Grate rind of orange and lemon. Cut orange and lemon into sections. Add the orange and lemon sections and rind; stir. Pour the mixture into quart jars and store in the refrigerator. Warm before serving over vanilla or butter pecan ice cream.

Makes 4 cups.

This recipe goes back to the time of Henry Clay and has been a favorite of family members.

Pomm-De-Terris

Pinch of salt
9 egg whites
1 teaspoon cream of tartar
1 1/4 cups sugar
1 cup cake flour, sifted
1 1/2 cups sugar
1 tablespoon white corn syrup
1/2 teaspoon salt
2 egg whites
1 teaspoon vanilla extract
1 cup finely chopped nuts
1 cup powdered sugar
2 tablespoons cinnamon

This dessert was a favorite of Miss Sally Shackelford who lived on West Main Street in Richmond. She often made the Pomm-De-Terris for various women's clubs and church groups for their dessert at their afternoon club meetings.

Add the salt to the 9 eggs white; beat until just beginning to become stiff. Add the cream of tartar and beat until stiff. Fold in the sugar, then the flour. Turn into two 8x8-inch pans lined with parchment paper. Bake at 350 degrees for 25 to 30 minutes. Cool. Combine the sugar, syrup, salt and 2 egg whites in a double boiler. Cook over medium heat, beating constantly for 7 minutes or until the frosting stands in peaks. Add the vanilla and nuts. Cut the cake into 2x1-inch pieces. Press and shape like a potato. Frost each piece and roll in powdered sugar and cinnamon. Place in cupcake papers to serve.

Makes 2 dozen.

Miss Burrier's White Fruit Cake

1 pound white raisins
1/2 pound citron, finely chopped
1/2 pound candied orange peel
1/2 pound candied pineapple
1/2 pound candied red cherries
1/2 pound candied green cherries
1 cup coconut
4 cups all-purpose flour, sifted
1 teaspoon baking powder
1/2 teaspoon baking soda
1/2 teaspoon salt
1 cup butter
1 1/2 cups sugar
1 tablespoon lemon juice
1 pound finely slivered, blanched almonds
10 egg whites, beaten stiff

Miss Mary Burrier was a home economics teacher at Eastern Kentucky State College for many years. My family lives across the road from her farm in Jessamine County. As a little girl, I remember going to her home in the summer with my grandmother. She always served the most delicious food. Her secret was fresh products—cream, butter and eggs from the farm. These were kept in the "cellar" until ready to use.

Combine the fruit in a large mixing bowl. Sift flour to measure, then sift together flour, baking powder, baking soda and salt in another bowl. Sift 3 times. Sift 1 cup of the flour mixture over the fruit. Cream the butter and gradually add the sugar; cream together thoroughly. Add the remaining flour to the creamed mixture. Beat until smooth. Add the lemon juice, fruits and nuts. Fold in the stiffly beaten egg whites. Pour into a coated, paper-lined tube pan. Bake at 250 degrees for 2 1/2 hours. Increase the oven temperature to 300 degrees and bake 15 minutes longer.

Makes one 6-pound cake.

appetizers & beverages

All roads in Richmond lead to the Bennett House. The landscape has changed drastically since this early Main Street scene. Whether folks are traveling North, South, East, or West, Richmond is a central point and the Bennett House always was and still is -- a great stopping off place.

Photo courtesy of Peggy Rice

Apple Walnut-Stuffed Celery Boats

2 stalks fresh, crisp celery
1/2 cup crumbled bleu cheese
1/4 cup toasted, finely chopped walnuts
1/2 cup finely chopped sweet apple
1 teaspoon lemon juice
Lettuce leaf
Mayonnaise to stick together

Cut the celery into 1 1/2-inch bite-size pieces. Combine the bleu cheese and walnuts in a medium bowl. Mix the lemon juice with the apple in a small bowl. Drain off any excess juice. Add the apple to the cheese mixture. Gently mix together. Place a small amount of the mixture onto each piece of celery. Place the celery on a leaf of lettuce and serve.

Hot Artichoke Dip

8-ounce package cream cheese, softened
1 cup mayonnaise
One or two 14-ounce jars artichoke hearts, drained and chopped
1 cup grated Parmesan cheese
1/2 cup shredded Cheddar cheese
2 shallots, finely chopped
1 clove garlic, finely chopped
Salt and pepper

Combine the cream cheese and mayonnaise in a bowl and mix until smooth. Add the artichokes, cheeses, shallots, garlic, salt and pepper. Spoon into a 1 1/2-quart baking dish. Bake at 350 degrees for 20 to 25 minutes. Serve with assorted crackers or toasted bread squares.

Artichoke Spread

12-ounce can unmarinated artichoke hearts, chopped
4 1/4-ounce can green chilies, diced
4 1/4-ounce can ripe olives, drained and chopped
1 cup mayonnaise
1 cup shredded Parmesan cheese
15 frozen miniature phyllo shells

Combine the artichokes, green chilies, olives, mayonnaise and Parmesan cheese in a large mixing bowl. Spoon the mixture evenly into the phyllo shells. Bake at 350 degrees for 8 to 10 minutes. Serve warm.

Makes 15.

Hot Artichoke Squares

1/3 cup chopped onion
1 clove garlic, minced
2 tablespoons bacon fat
4 eggs, beaten until frothy
14-ounce can artichoke hearts, drained and chopped
1/4 cup dry bread crumbs
1/2 pound shredded Swiss cheese
2 tablespoons minced parsley
1/2 teaspoon salt
Pepper to taste
1/4 teaspoon oregano
1/8 teaspoon hot sauce

Sauté the onion and garlic in the bacon fat in a skillet until tender. Combine with the remaining ingredients in a large mixing bowl. Bake in a coated 7x11-inch baking dish at 325 degrees for 30 minutes. Cut into 1 1/2-inch squares to serve.

This dish can be made and cooked in advance, storing in the refrigerator up to 1 week or freezing. To serve, reheat in microwave.

Avocado-Feta Salsa

2 plum tomatoes, chopped
1 avocado, peeled, halved, seeded and chopped
1/4 cup finely chopped red onion
1 clove garlic, minced
1 tablespoon snipped fresh parsley
1 tablespoon snipped fresh oregano
1 tablespoon olive oil
1 tablespoon red or white wine vinegar
4 ounces coarsely crumbled feta cheese
Pita bread or tortilla chips

Combine the tomatoes, avocado, onion, garlic, parsley, oregano, olive oil, vinegar and feta cheese in a medium bowl. Mix well. Cover and chill for 2 hours. Serve with pita bread or tortilla chips.

Bacon Roll-ups

1/2 to 3/4 cup boiling water
2 tablespoons butter, melted
3/4 cup golden raisins and cherries
2 cups herb-seasoned stuffing mix
1 egg, beaten
1/4 pound ground beef
1/4 pound ground hot sausage
1/2 cup shredded Cheddar cheese
1 pound bacon slices, cut into fourths, optional

Combine the water, butter, raisins, cherries and stuffing mix in a mixing bowl. Stir until thoroughly moistened. Add the egg, beef, sausage and cheese. Mix well. Shape the mixture into oblong balls and wrap one piece of the bacon around each. Place on a baking sheet and bake at 375 degrees for 30 minutes. Drain on paper towels. Omit bacon to reduce calories.

Makes 3 1/2 dozen.

Baby Hot Browns

24 slices party rye bread
3 tablespoons butter or margarine
3 tablespoons flour
1 cup milk
1 1/2 cups shredded Cheddar cheese
1 1/2 cups cooked, diced turkey
1/4 teaspoon salt
1/4 teaspoon red pepper
1/2 cup grated Parmesan cheese
6 slices bacon, cooked and crumbled
5 plum tomatoes, sliced

Arrange the bread slices on a lightly coated baking sheet. Broil 6 inches from the heat for 3 to 4 minutes. Set aside. Melt the butter in a microwave and add the flour. Cook 1 to 2 minutes or until smooth. Whisk the milk in gradually. Cook 1 to 2 minutes or until thick. Add the Cheddar cheese. Stir in the turkey, salt and red pepper. Top the bread evenly with the mixture. Sprinkle evenly with Parmesan cheese and half the bacon. Bake at 500 degrees for 2 minutes or until the Parmesan cheese is melted. Top with the tomato slices and remaining bacon.

Makes 24 servings.

Sausage Quiches

1/4 pound ground hot pork sausage
1/4 cup minced celery
3 tablespoons minced onion
3 large eggs, lightly beaten
3/4 cup half-and-half
1/2 cup finely shredded mozzarella cheese
1/2 teaspoon poultry seasoning
1/4 teaspoon salt
1/4 teaspoon ground pepper
1/8 teaspoon rubbed sage
15 frozen miniature phyllo shells
Fresh parsley for garnish

Cook the sausage, celery and onion in a skillet over medium-high heat for 8 minutes, stirring occasionally, or until the sausage is finely crumbled and no longer pink. Combine the sausage mixture, eggs, half-and-half, cheese, poultry seasoning, salt, pepper and sage in a medium bowl. Mix well. Spoon the mixture evenly into the shells. Bake at 350 degrees for 15 minutes or until set. Garnish with fresh parsley, if desired. Serve warm.

Makes 15 mini quiches.

Stuffed Mushrooms

24 large mushrooms
2 cloves garlic, minced
1 stick butter
1 cup bread crumbs
1/2 cup grated Parmesan cheese
1/2 teaspoon salt
1/4 teaspoon pepper
2 tablespoons chopped parsley

Remove the mushroom stems. Chop the stems fine and sauté in a skillet with the garlic and 4 tablespoons of butter. Add the bread crumbs, Parmesan cheese, salt, pepper and parsley. Pack the mushroom caps with the stuffing and place on a baking sheet. Melt the remaining butter and pour over the mushrooms. Bake at 370 degrees for 15 minutes. Serve in a chafing dish to keep warm.

Makes 24.

Herb Cheese Cake

1 1/4 cups all-purpose flour
1 1/2 cups unsalted butter, chilled
1/2 teaspoon salt
1 large egg yolk
2 teaspoons lemon zest
2 cloves garlic
1 large onion, coarsely chopped
2/3 cup fresh chopped parsley
3/4 cup grated Parmesan cheese
Two 8-ounce packages cream cheese, at room temperature
3 tablespoons all-purpose flour
4 large eggs
2 teaspoons salt
1/2 teaspoon hot sauce
2 tablespoons lemon juice
1 teaspoon dried oregano
1 teaspoon tarragon
1/2 teaspoon rosemary
1/2 cup chopped pepperoni
Crackers
Grapes and mint leaves for garnish

Blend the flour, butter, salt, egg yolk and lemon zest in a food processor to oatmeal consistency. Remove and knead lightly. Shape into a ball. Wrap in waxed paper and refrigerate until slightly chilled. Spread 1/3 of the dough evenly in the bottom of an 8-inch spring form pan. Press the remaining dough around the sides. Store in the refrigerator while preparing the filling. Chop the garlic in a food processor. Add the onion, parsley and Parmesan cheese. Add the cream cheese, one package at a time, and process. Add the flour and 1 egg. Process until smooth. Add the remaining eggs, one at a time, blending well. Add the salt, hot sauce, lemon juice and herbs. Fold in the pepperoni and pour into dough-lined pan. Bake at 400 degrees for 10 minutes. Reduce the heat to 325 degrees and bake 50 minutes longer. Let stand 1 hour before serving. Serve on a silver tray with crackers. Garnish with fresh grapes and mint leaves. The cheesecake can be frozen, then warmed in a 300-degree oven for 30 minutes after thawed to room temperature.

This recipe was given to me by a cousin, Patsy Rich, from Georgetown, Kentucky. She serves it at many events and when she entertains. It's marvelous for parties.

Apricot Balls

8-ounce package cream cheese
7 ounces flaked coconut
3-ounce package apricot gelatin
1 tablespoon sugar
1 cup chopped walnuts or pecans

Combine all the ingredients in a mixing bowl. Chill until firm. Roll into 1-inch balls. Chill in a single layer until firm. Cover tightly and store in the refrigerator.

Makes 30 balls.

Chocolate Chip Cheese Ball

8-ounce package cream cheese
1/2 cup butter, softened
1/4 teaspoon vanilla extract
3/4 cup powdered sugar
2 tablespoons brown sugar
3/4 cup chocolate chips
3/4 cup chopped pecans
5 1/2-ounce can crushed pineapple, drained
Sugar cookies or vanilla wafers

Combine the cream cheese, butter and vanilla in a mixing bowl. Blend until fluffy. Add the sugars and mix well. Fold in the chocolate chips. Cover and refrigerate 2 hours. Shape the dough into a ball. Cover with plastic wrap and refrigerate 1 hour. Uncover and roll in the pecans before serving. Garnish with the crushed pineapple. Serve with sugar cookies or vanilla wafers.

Makes about 2 cups.

Charmin' Cherry Cheese Ball

1/2 cup butter, softened
1 cup grated Cheddar cheese
8-ounce package cream cheese
3 green onions, chopped
1 cup real bacon bits
12-ounce jar cherry preserves
Crackers

Combine the butter, Cheddar cheese and cream cheese in a mixing bowl. Shape the mixture into a ball. Roll in the onion and bacon bits. Chill. Pulse preserves in a blender for a few seconds. Pour over the cheese ball just before serving. Serve with crackers.

This cheese ball is beautiful for a holiday table.

White Chocolate Covered Apple Slices

4 to 5 Granny Smith or Red Delicious apples
2 tablespoons lemon juice
2 cups water
White melting chocolate bars or bits
1/2 cup finely chopped walnuts or pecans

Slice the unpeeled apples, using a round apple corer/slicer, then slice each slice once more using a sharp knife. Place the slices in a mixture of the lemon juice and water to prevent apples from turning brown. Drain well on a white paper towel. The apples must be dry before dipping in the chocolate. Melt the chocolate in a microwave following the instructions on the package. Dip each apple slice in the chocolate up to the peel. Place the slices on waxed paper and sprinkle with the nuts before the chocolate hardens. Store the apples in a tin with waxed paper between the layers in the refrigerator up to 2 or 3 days.

Makes 48 slices.

Cranberry-Lemon Tea

8 cups water
4 regular-size tea bags
1 cinnamon stick
1 1/4 cups sugar
4 cups cranberry juice cocktail
1/4 cups lemon juice
Cinnamon sticks

Bring the water to a boil in a tea kettle. Pour the boiling water over the tea bags and cinnamon stick in a large container. Steep for 5 minutes. Remove the tea bags and cinnamon. Add the sugar, stirring until dissolved. Stir in the cranberry juice cocktail and lemon juice. Place over a medium heat until the mixture is heated through. Serve with cinnamon sticks.

Applewood Julep

1 cup pineapple juice
1 cup orange juice
1/4 cup lemon juice
1 quart apple juice

Combine all the ingredients in a large pitcher. Serve chilled.

Serves 6.

Tea Punch

5 tablespoons loose tea or 5 family-style tea bags
2 quarts hot water
8 cups sugar
1 quart lemon juice
1 quart orange juice
1 quart grapefruit/pineapple juice
10 quarts ice water
1 quart ginger ale

Place the tea in hot water. Steep 5 minutes; strain or remove the tea bags. Add the sugar, stirring until dissolved. Cool. Add the juices and water. Mix well. Stir in the ginger ale just before serving.

Makes 100 cups.

Banana Slush Punch

5 to 6 bananas, halved
46-ounce can pineapple juice
2 to 3 cups sugar
6 cups warm water
12-ounce can frozen lemonade, thawed
Two 12-ounce cans frozen orange juice, thawed
4 liters ginger ale

Blend the bananas with the pineapple juice in a blender. Combine the banana mixture with the sugar, water and frozen juices in a large bowl. Mix well. Pour the mixture into 3 or 4 plastic containers, 3/4 full. Contents expand when frozen. Freeze 2 to 3 days before serving. Let the punch thaw 1 hour before serving. Chop in big hunks and place in a punch bowl. Add the ginger ale and stir until it becomes slushy. Add the ginger ale to thin as needed.

Makes 50 cups.

This is the all-time favorite punch at Bennett House events. Men, women, old and young always ask for two or three glasses. "This punch is wonderful – delicious!" is the comment.

Champagne Punch

3 cups red fruit punch, chilled
3 cups pineapple juice, chilled
3 cups white grape juice, chilled
1 bottle pink champagne or
two 12-ounce cans ginger ale

Stir all the ingredients into a large punch bowl. Serve chilled.

Fruited Tea Punch

64 ounces tea, sweetened
32 ounces orange juice
32 ounces ginger ale

Combine the tea and orange juice. Gently stir in the ginger ale just before serving.

Serves 12 to 15.

Holiday Cranberry Punch

32-ounce bottle unsweetened orange-pineapple juice
32-ounce bottle cranberry juice cocktail
1/4 cup sugar
3 whole cloves
2 cinnamon sticks
Orange slices

Combine all the ingredients in a crock-pot or large pan. Heat. Remove the cloves and cinnamon sticks before serving. Serve warm and top with the orange slices, if desired.

Makes 8 cups.

Cranberry Pineapple Punch

48-ounce bottle cranberry juice
48-ounce can pineapple juice
1/2 cup sugar
2 teaspoons almond extract
2-liter bottle ginger ale, chilled

Combine the cranberry juice, pineapple juice, sugar and almond extract until the sugar is dissolved. Cover and chill 8 hours. Stir in the ginger ale before serving.

Ruby Red Slush

Two 6-ounce cans frozen orange juice concentrate, thawed
4 1/2 cups water
Two 46-ounce cans red fruit punch
46-ounce can unsweetened pineapple juice
48-ounce bottle cranapple juice
Two 33.8-ounce bottles ginger ale, chilled

Combine the thawed orange juice concentrate and water in a large bowl. Mix well. Stir in the fruit punch, pineapple juice and cranapple juice. Pour the mixture into plastic containers, 3/4 full and freeze. Contents expands when frozen. Remove from the freezer and partially thaw. Add the ginger ale and make slush to serve.

Apple Cider Tea

8 cups water
3 family-size tea bags
3 to 4 cinnamon sticks
1 lemon, thinly sliced
3/4 cup sugar
1/2 gallon apple cider

Combine the water, tea bags, cinnamon sticks and lemon in a large saucepan. Bring to a boil. Reduce the heat and simmer for 20 minutes. Remove the tea bags, cinnamon sticks and lemon. Add the sugar. Stir until the sugar completely dissolves. Pour in the apple cider and heat through.

Makes 24 cups.

Spicy Autumn Cider

4 cups boiling water
2 tea bags
1 quart apple cider
1 cup brown sugar
1 stick cinnamon
1/8 teaspoon nutmeg
1/8 teaspoon allspice
2 cups fresh orange juice
1 cup lemon juice

Combine and mix all the ingredients in a large bowl. Pour into a crock-pot or large coffee pot. Serve hot.

Makes 10 to 12 servings.

Richmond Eggnog

6 eggs, separated and beaten
1 cup sugar
1 pint whisky
1 quart heavy whipping cream

Pour the beaten egg yolks into a bowl. Add 2/3 cup of the sugar and beat and beat and beat. They should be thick and lemon-colored no matter how your arm aches for relief. Slowly add the whisky, beating continuously. When this much of your task is completed set aside and turn your attention to the whites.

Beat the egg whites until stiff but not dry and add the remaining sugar, beating it in as you would making a meringue. Slowly pour the whisky mixture into the whites, folding it in gently. If you do this the eggnog will not separate. Whip the cream and fold it into the eggnog mixture. Even if you have been doing this by hand, you'll not be too exhausted to stand back and admire the bowl of "fluff" you have produced.

This eggnog was served to many "old Richmond families" throughout the years. The Bennett House often hosts the Society of Boonesborough holiday reception. I chose a more modern version of Creamy Nog Punch. It's not nearly as hard on the "old body." Some say it's better than a pile of presents! Sometimes the men sneak in a little Kentucky bourbon while I'm not looking.

Creamy Nog Punch

1 gallon vanilla ice cream
1/2 gallon prepared eggnog
1 teaspoon nutmeg
1/2 teaspoon cinnamon
16-ounce container frozen whipped topping, thawed

Scoop the ice cream into a punch bowl. Pour the eggnog over ice cream and sprinkle with the nutmeg and cinnamon. Gently stir in the whipped topping. Serve immediately. Stir as needed.

Makes 1 1/2 gallons.

breads & breakfast

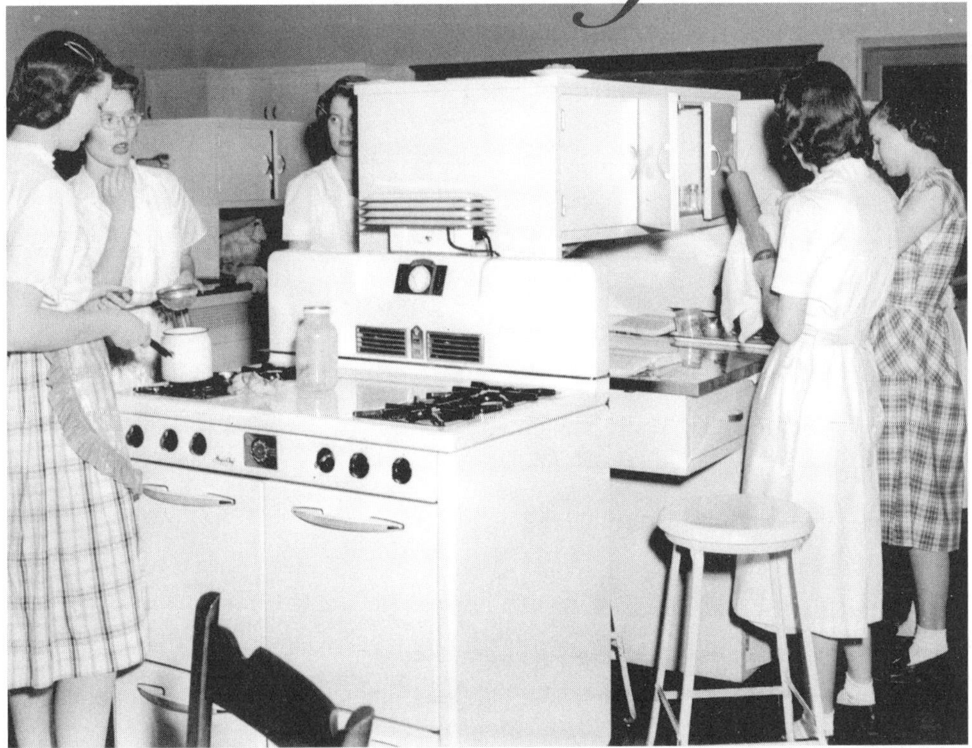

I learned the secrets of baking and fine cooking as a home economics major at Eastern Kentucky University. There were no quick methods, prepackaged or three ingredient recipes in those days. We tried and tested many recipes in the foods lab at the old Fitzpatrick building. The Mary K. Burrier building, complete with modern kitchens and equipment, opened my senior year. I always dreamed of a state-of-the-art, upscale, efficient kitchen. I am still dreaming, but I seem to do my best cooking the old-fashioned way in the Bennett House kitchen.

Photo courtesy of Eastern Kentucky University Archives, Richmond, Kentucky

Strawberry Nut Bread

3 cups self-rising flour
2 cups sugar
3 eggs, well-beaten
1 cup oil
21-ounce can strawberry pie filling
1 cup chopped pecans

Combine the flour and sugar in a large mixing bowl. Make a well. Add the eggs and oil. Stir until moist. Add the pie filling and chopped pecans. Mix well. Pour into 3 small or 2 regular coated and floured bread pans. Bake at 350 degrees for 1 hour or until done. Or use mini pans and bake 20 to 25 minutes at 350 degrees. Serve with strawberry cream cheese.

Whipped Strawberry Butter

1/2 pound butter or margarine, softened
10-ounce package frozen strawberries, thawed and drained
1/2 cup powdered sugar

Place all of the ingredients in a mixing bowl and blend until smooth. Serve at room temperature.

Best Ever Banana Bread

1 cup sugar
1/2 cup butter or margarine, melted
2 eggs
1 cup mashed bananas
2 cups all-purpose flour
1 teaspoon salt
1/2 teaspoon baking soda
1/4 cup buttermilk
1/2 cup chopped nuts

Combine the ingredients in a mixing bowl. Pour into two coated and floured loaf pans. Bake at 350 degrees for 50 minutes.

Apricot Pecan Bread

1/4 cup butter or margarine, softened
1 1/4 cups sugar
1 egg, beaten
2 cups all-purpose flour, sifted
1/2 teaspoon baking powder
1/2 teaspoon baking soda
1/2 teaspoon salt
1 tablespoon coriander
1 cup canned apricots, drained and mashed
2 tablespoons sour cream
1/2 teaspoon almond extract
1/2 cup chopped pecans
1/2 cup maraschino cherries, halved

Beat the butter and sugar in a large bowl. Stir in the egg. Combine the flour, baking powder, baking soda, salt and coriander in another bowl. Stir into the sugar mixture. Fold in the apricots, sour cream and almond extract. Stir in the pecans and cherries. Pour into a coated and floured pan. Bake at 350 degrees for 50 minutes. Cool 5 minutes before removing from the pan. Wrap and refrigerate 24 hours before serving.

Autumn Pumpkin Bread

2 1/4 cups all-purpose flour
1 tablespoon pumpkin pie spice
2 teaspoons baking powder
1/2 teaspoon salt
2 eggs
2 cups sugar
15-ounce can pumpkin
1/2 cup oil
1 cup cranberries, optional

Combine the flour, pumpkin pie spice, baking powder and salt in a large mixing bowl; set aside. Blend the eggs, sugar, pumpkin and oil in another bowl. Add to the flour mixture. Stir just until moistened. Fold in the cranberries. Spoon the batter into 2 coated and floured 9x5-inch loaf pans. Bake at 350 degrees for 55 to 60 minutes or until a toothpick inserted near the center comes out clean. Cool in the pans for 5 to 10 minutes. Remove from the pans; cool completely.

Pineapple Bread

1/2 cup margarine, softened, or scant 1/2 cup oil
1 cup sugar
2 eggs
2 cups all-purpose flour
2 teaspoons baking powder
1/2 teaspoon salt
8-ounce can crushed pineapple, undrained
1 teaspoon vanilla extract

Cream the margarine in a mixing bowl. Gradually add the sugar. Beat well. Add the eggs one at a time, beating well after each addition. Combine the flour, baking powder and salt in a medium bowl. Add to the creamed mixture alternately with the pineapple, mixing well after each addition. Stir in the vanilla. Spoon the batter into a coated and floured loaf pan. Bake at 350 degrees for 55 to 60 minutes or until a toothpick inserted near the center comes out clean. Cool 10 minutes in the pan before removing.

Poppy Seed Bread

3 eggs
3/4 cup oil
2 1/4 cups sugar
3 cups all-purpose flour
1 1/2 teaspoons salt
1 1/2 teaspoons baking powder
1 1/2 cup milk
1 1/2 teaspoons almond extract
1 1/2 teaspoons butter or lemon flavoring
1 1/2 teaspoons vanilla extract
1 1/2 teaspoons poppy seeds

Beat the eggs, oil and sugar in a mixing bowl. Sift the flour, salt and baking powder in another bowl. Add alternately with the milk to the egg mixture. Add the flavorings and poppy seeds. Pour into coated loaf pans. Bake at 350 degrees for 1 hour or 30 minutes for smaller pans. Glaze while bread is warm.

Poppy Seed Bread Glaze

1/4 cup orange juice
3/4 cup sugar
1/2 teaspoon almond extract
1/2 teaspoon vanilla extract

Combine all of the ingredients and mix well. Pour over the warm Poppy Seed Bread.

Spicy Pumpkin Bread

3 cups all-purpose flour
1 teaspoon baking soda
1 teaspoon salt
1 tablespoon cinnamon
1 tablespoon pumpkin pie spice
2 cups sugar
2 cups pumpkin
4 eggs
1 1/4 cups oil
1 cup chopped nuts, optional

Combine the dry ingredients in a large bowl. Combine the pumpkin, eggs, oil and nuts in another bowl. Add to the flour mixture. Mix thoroughly. Pour into two 8 1/2x4 1/2-inch coated and floured pans. Bake at 350 degrees for 45 to 60 minutes or until a toothpick inserted near the center comes out clean.

Makes 2 loaves.

Bennett House Spoon Bread

1 cup yellow or white cornmeal
1 teaspoon salt
1 teaspoon baking powder
1/2 teaspoon baking soda
1/4 cup butter or margarine
2 cups buttermilk or soured milk
4 large eggs

Mix the cornmeal, salt, baking powder and baking soda. The dry ingredients can be prepared up to this point 3 days ahead and stored tightly covered at room temperature. Place the butter in a deep 1 1/2-quart baking dish and set in a 375-degree oven. Heat until hot and bubbly, about 6 to 8 minutes. Whisk the buttermilk or soured milk with the eggs in a medium bowl until well blended. Add the cornmeal mixture and whisk until blended. Remove the baking dish from the oven and carefully tilt to coat the bottom and sides with melted butter. Pour the excess butter into the cornmeal batter and whisk to blend. Pour the batter into the baking dish. Bake 30 minutes or until puffed and browned on top. Let stand at room temperature for 5 minutes before serving.

To make soured milk, mix 2 cups milk with 2 tablespoons cider vinegar. Let stand 5 minutes until thickened and small curds have formed.

Makes 8 servings.

Madison County Spoon Bread

3 cups milk
1 1/4 cups cornmeal
3 eggs, well-beaten
2 tablespoons butter, melted
1 3/4 teaspoon baking powder
1 teaspoon salt

Bring the milk to a boil in a saucepan. Stir in the cornmeal and cook until very thick, stirring constantly. Remove from the heat and allow to cool. The batter will be very stiff. Add the eggs, butter, baking powder and salt. Beat with electric mixer. If beating by hand, beat 10 minutes with a wooden spoon. Pour into a well-coated baking dish. Bake at 325 degrees for 30 minutes.

Broccoli Cornbread

4 eggs, beaten
1 medium onion, chopped
Two 8-ounce boxes corn muffin mix
1 stick butter, melted
10 ounces chopped broccoli, cooked and drained
11-ounce can cream-style corn

Combine all the ingredients in a large mixing bowl. Pour into a coated 9x13-inch baking dish. Bake at 350 degrees for 50 minutes.

Bennett House Signature Scones

2 cups all-purpose flour
2 teaspoons baking powder
1/4 teaspoon salt
2 tablespoons sugar
1/4 teaspoon baking soda
1 teaspoon grated orange rind
6 teaspoons unsalted butter, softened 10 seconds in microwave
1/2 cup buttermilk
2 eggs
1 tablespoon milk

Combine the flour, baking powder, salt, sugar, baking soda and orange rind with a pastry blender. Cut in the butter until the mixture resembles coarse crumbs. Mix the buttermilk and 1 egg in small bowl. Add to the flour mixture. Stir until soft ball forms. Turn out on a floured surface and knead 2 or 3 times. Roll out and cut to desired shape using a cookie cutter. Place on a baking sheet lined with parchment paper. Combine 1 egg and milk in a small bowl. Brush onto the scones. Bake at 370 degrees for 10 to 15 minutes or until brown.

Makes 1 dozen scones.

Signature Scones with Lemon Curd

Traditional English Scones

4 cups plus 1 tablespoon all-purpose flour
2 tablespoons sugar, plus extra for sprinkling
2 tablespoons baking powder
2 teaspoons kosher salt
3/4 pound cold unsalted butter, diced
5 eggs, lightly beaten
1 cup cold heavy cream
3/4 cup raisins
2 tablespoons milk or water

Combine the 4 cups of flour, 2 tablespoons sugar, baking powder and salt in an electric mixer fitted with a paddle attachment. Blend in the butter at the lowest speed and mix until the butter is in pea-size pieces. Combine 4 eggs and the cream; quickly add to the flour mixture. Combine just until blended. Combine the raisins and 1 tablespoon flour; add to the dough and mix quickly. The dough may be a bit sticky. Place the dough on a floured surface, making sure the dough is well combined. After flouring a rolling pin and hands, roll the dough to 3/4-inch to 1-inch thick. You will see lumps of butter in the dough. Cut into squares with a 4-inch cutter then cut in half diagonally to make triangles. Place on a baking sheet lined with parchment paper. Combine 1 egg and 2 tablespoons of milk or water and brush on top of the scones. Sprinkle with the extra sugar. Bake at 400 degrees for 20 to 25 minutes or until the outsides are crisp and insides are done.

Gingerbread Scones

2 cups all-purpose flour
2 teaspoons baking powder
1/2 teaspoon salt
1/4 teaspoon baking soda
1/3 cup dark brown sugar, packed
3/4 teaspoon ground cinnamon
1/2 teaspoon ground ginger
1/8 teaspoon ground cloves
6 tablespoons unsalted butter
2/3 cup currants
1/2 cup buttermilk
1 egg
1 teaspoon vanilla extract
1 egg white

Combine the flour, baking powder, salt, baking soda, brown sugar, cinnamon, ginger and cloves in a large bowl. Cut in the butter with a pastry blender until the mixture resembles coarse crumbs. Mix in the currants. Whisk the buttermilk, egg, and vanilla in a small bowl until combined. Pour into the dry mixture. Quickly stir together until a soft dough forms. Place on a lightly floured surface and turn over 5 to 6 times. Roll the dough 1/2-inch thick using a floured rolling pin. Cut into 4-inch squares, then cut in half diagonally to make triangles. Place on a large baking sheet lightly coated or lined with parchment paper. Brush the tops with egg white. Bake at 400 degrees for 10 to 12 minutes or until lightly brown. Serve with Lemon Curd.

Makes 12 scones.

Lemon Curd

3 eggs
1/2 cup lemon juice
1/2 cup butter, melted
1 cup sugar

Place the eggs in a microwavable bowl and beat until frothy. Stir in the lemon juice, butter and sugar. Microwave on high for 6 minutes, stirring every two minutes. Remove from the microwave oven and stir until smooth. Cool and store in the refrigerator up to two weeks. Serve cold or at room temperature with hot scones.
To make using regular stove, place all the ingredients in a double boiler over boiling water for 20 minutes, stirring constantly until thick.

Makes 2 cups.

Petite Pecan Muffins

2 eggs
1 cup brown sugar
1/3 cup butter, melted
1 teaspoon vanilla extract
1/2 cup all-purpose flour
1 cup chopped pecans

Beat the eggs in a mixing bowl. Add the sugar, margarine and vanilla. Stir in the flour and nuts. Pour into well-coated, small muffin tins. Fill half full. Bake at 350 degrees for 12 to 15 minutes.

Makes 3 dozen.

Wild Plum Muffins

2 cups self-rising flour
2 cups sugar
2 teaspoons allspice
1 cup chopped walnuts
Two 4-ounce jars baby food plums
3 large eggs
1 cup oil

Combine the dry ingredients in a large mixing bowl. Add the plums, eggs and oil. Stir until mixed well. Fill mini muffin pans half full. Bake at 350 degrees for 15 to 20 minutes.

Makes 90 mini muffins.

Tea Pot Fountain

Banana Muffins

3 to 4 bananas
1 cup sugar
1/4 cup oil
1 egg
1 cup all-purpose flour
1 cup whole wheat flour
1/3 cup wheat germ
1 teaspoon baking soda
1 teaspoon baking powder
1/2 teaspoon salt
1 teaspoon vanilla extract
1/2 cup chopped nuts

Mash the bananas in a large bowl. Add the sugar, oil and egg; mix well. Add the flour, wheat germ, baking soda, baking powder, salt, vanilla and nuts. Mix thoroughly. Spoon into a paper-lined muffin tins. Bake at 350 degrees for 20 minutes.

English Muffin French Toast

1/4 cup egg substitute
1 cup milk
1 teaspoon vanilla extract
6 English muffins, split
Kiwi, peeled and chopped
1 cup blueberries
1 cup strawberries, chopped
1 cup chopped nectarines
Pancake syrup
Fresh mint springs for garnish

Combine the egg substitute, milk and vanilla in a mixing bowl. Pour into a gallon-size plastic bag. Add the English muffins. Seal and chill 8 hours, turning occasionally. Remove the muffins from the bag. Cook the muffins in a large skillet coated with cooking spray over medium heat for 2 to 3 minutes or until golden brown. Top with the fruit and syrup. Garnish with mint sprigs.

Macadamia Nut French Toast

4 large eggs, lightly beaten
1/4 cup sugar
1/4 teaspoon ground nutmeg
2/3 cup orange juice
1/3 cup milk
1/2 teaspoon vanilla extract
16-ounce loaf Italian bread, cut into 1-inch slices
2/3 cup butter, melted
1/2 cup chopped macadamia nuts
Powdered sugar and ground nutmeg for garnish

Combine the eggs, sugar, nutmeg, orange juice, milk and vanilla in medium bowl. Mix well. Place the bread slices in a single layer into a lightly coated 9x13-inch baking dish. Pour the egg mixture over the bread slices. Cover and refrigerate 8 hours or overnight, turning the bread once. Pour the butter into a 15x10x1-inch jelly roll pan; place the bread slices in a single layer in the pan. Bake at 400 degrees for 10 minutes. Sprinkle with the nuts and bake 10 additional minutes. Garnish with powdered sugar and nutmeg, if desired, and serve immediately with maple syrup.

Serves 6.

This is the all-time favorite breakfast item served at the Bennett House. Repeat guests always ask if they can have it.

Whipping Cream Biscuits

1 cup butter or margarine
4 cups self-rising flour
1 3/4 to 2 cups whipping cream
1/2 cup butter or margarine, melted

Cut the butter into the flour using a pastry blender or fork until the mixture resembles coarse crumbs. Add the whipping cream, stirring just until the dry ingredients are moistened. Place the dough on a lightly floured surface and knead lightly 3 to 4 times. Roll or pat the dough to 3/4-inch thickness. Cut with a biscuit cutter and place on a lightly coated baking sheet. Bake at 400 degrees for 13 to 15 minutes. Brush with melted butter.

Makes 2 dozen.

Sweet Potato Biscuits

3 cups all-purpose flour
3/4 cup sugar
1 tablespoon salt
3 teaspoons baking powder
1 1/2 teaspoons allspice
1 teaspoon cinnamon
3/4 cup shortening
2 cups mashed sweet potatoes
1/3 cup milk

Mix the dry ingredients in a large bowl. Cut in the shortening using a pastry blender until the mixture resembles coarse crumbs. Stir in the sweet potatoes. Add the milk, stirring just until the ingredients are moistened. Place the dough onto a floured surface and roll to 1/2-inch thickness. Cut the dough using a 2-inch biscuit cutter. Place on a lightly coated baking sheet. Bake at 450 degrees for 12 to 15 minutes.

Makes 18 to 20 biscuits.

Angel Biscuits

2 3/4 cups all-purpose flour
1 1/2 teaspoons baking powder
1/2 teaspoon baking soda
1 teaspoon salt
2 tablespoons sugar
1/2 cup shortening
1 1/2 teaspoons yeast, dissolved in 2 tablespoons warm water
1 cup buttermilk, at room temperature

Sift the dry ingredients into a large bowl. Cut in the shortening using a pastry blender until the mixture resembles coarse crumbs. Combine the yeast and buttermilk in a small bowl. Add the buttermilk mixture to the dry ingredients until a dough is formed. Place on a lightly floured surface and roll 1/2-inch thick with a rolling pin. Cut into small rounds. Place on a lightly coated baking sheet. Bake at 450 degrees for 12 to 14 minutes or until lightly browned.

Processor Beaten Biscuits

2 1/2 cups all-purpose flour
1/2 teaspoon baking powder
1/2 teaspoon salt
1 teaspoon sugar
1/3 cup shortening
1/4 cup water, plus 2 ice cubes
1/4 cup milk

Combine the dry ingredients in a processor. Add the shortening and process until the mixture resembles course crumbs. Add the liquid, except ice, in a stream until the mixture forms into a ball. Divide in half and process each half 2 minutes with 1 ice cube. Put back together. Place on a floured surface and roll to 1/4-inch thick. Fold and roll again several times until smooth, about 5 minutes. Cut into rounds. Prick the tops with a fork. Bake at 350 degrees for 25 minutes.

Makes 2 dozen.

Quick Cheese Biscuits

2 cups buttermilk baking mix
2/3 cup milk
1/2 to 1 cup shredded Cheddar cheese
1/4 cup margarine
1/2 teaspoon garlic powder
1 tablespoon parsley flakes

Mix the baking mix, milk and cheese in a large bowl until a soft dough forms. Beat for 30 seconds. Drop by spoonfuls onto an uncoated baking sheet. Bake at 450 degrees for 10 minutes or until light brown. Combine the margarine, garlic powder and parsley flakes and brush over the warm biscuits before removing from the baking sheet. Serve warm.

Spoon Rolls

1/4-ounce package dry yeast
2 cups warm water
1 1/2 sticks margarine, melted
1/4 cup sugar
1 egg, beaten
4 cups self-rising flour

Stir the yeast into the water. Cream the butter and sugar in a large mixing bowl. Add the egg. Mix well. Add the dissolved yeast. Gradually add the flour and stir until mixed well. Place in an airtight container and refrigerate. Drop by teaspoonfuls on a well-coated baking pan to cook. Bake at 350 degrees for 20 minutes.

Makes 2 dozen rolls.

This is a great recipe when in a hurry or first learning to cook. The rolls are light and so tasty.

Margaret Hunter's Yeast Rolls

1/2 cup shortening
1/4 cup sugar
1/2 cup hot water
1/2 cup cold water
1/4-ounce package dry yeast
1 egg, beaten
3 cups all-purpose flour
2 tablespoons margarine, melted

Cream the shortening and sugar in a mixing bowl. Add the hot water, cold water and yeast, mixing well after each addition. Add the egg. Mix well. Stir in the flour. Cover and refrigerate for 8 hours. Melt the margarine in a glass or aluminum pie pan. Roll the dough 1/2-inch thick with rolling pin. Cut out rounds with a biscuit cutter and dip in the melted margarine. Place in the baking pie pan. Cover and place in a warm place to rise, about 30 minutes. Bake at 350 degrees for 20 to 25 minutes or until golden.

This is my mother's recipe. She always made them for special occasions and holiday events.

Rich Yeast Rolls

1 cup milk
1/4 cup butter or margarine
1/2 cup warm water
5 1/2 cups all-purpose flour, unsifted
1/4 cup sugar
1 1/2 teaspoons salt
Two 1/4-ounce packages dry yeast
1 egg, beaten

Scald the milk in a saucepan. Stir in the margarine and water. Cool to lukewarm. Mix 2 cups flour, sugar, salt and yeast thoroughly in a large bowl. Add the liquids gradually to the dry ingredients. Add the egg. Beat at a medium speed for 2 minutes. Add 1/2 cup flour and beat at a high speed for 2 minutes. Stir in the additional flour to make a soft dough. Turn out onto a floured surface and knead until smooth and elastic. Place in a coated bowl, turning once to coat top. Cover and let rise in a warm place until the dough doubles in size. Punch down. Pinch off dough the size of a marble, roll into a ball and place three pieces in each coated muffin pan. Cover and let rise, about 20 minutes. Bake at 375 degrees for 20 to 25 minutes or until golden.

Cheese Straws

8 ounces sharp Cheddar cheese, grated
1 stick butter, softened
1 1/2 cups all-purpose flour, unsifted
1 teaspoon baking powder
1 teaspoon salt
1/4 teaspoon red pepper

Combine the cheese and butter in a large mixing bowl. Add the remaining ingredients and mix well by hand. Place the dough in a cookie press. Use the small center star insert to push out two-inch straws. Bake on an uncoated cookie sheet or baking stone at 375 degrees for 10 to 12 minutes.

Makes 7 to 8 dozen straws.

Yesterday is History
Tomorrow is a Mystery
Today is a Gift,
That's why we call it "the Present."

Breakfast Bread Pudding

2 cups milk
2 eggs
1/3 cup brown sugar, firmly packed
3/4 teaspoon vanilla extract
1/4 teaspoon salt
4 cups dry bread cubes
15-ounce can pear halves or slices, drained and chopped
1/8 teaspoon cinnamon
1 cup granola

Combine the milk, eggs, brown sugar, vanilla and salt in a large bowl; add the bread cubes. Pour the mixture into a lightly coated 8x8-inch pan. Arrange the pears over the bread; sprinkle with the cinnamon and top with the granola. Bake at 350 degrees for 50 to 60 minutes or until a knife inserted near the center comes out clean. Let sit for 5 minutes before serving. Serve warm.

Makes 6 servings.

Breakfast Banana Split

1 banana
1/2 cup crunchy cereal, grape nuts or granola
1/2 cup fruit-flavored yogurt
1/4 cup blueberries or sliced strawberries
1/4 cup pineapple chunks, drained
Maraschino cherries, optional

Peel the banana and cut down the middle lengthwise with a butter knife. Place the banana in a cereal bowl or banana split dish. Sprinkle half of the cereal over the banana. Spoon the yogurt over the banana and cereal. Add the rest of the cereal and top with the fruit. Add the cherries, if desired.

Baked Fruit Compote

16 ounces pitted, sweet dark cherries in juice
1/4 cup brown sugar, firmly packed
1 tablespoon cornstarch
2 tablespoons lemon juice
1/4 cup orange juice
29-ounce can sliced peaches, drained, reserving juice
6 ounces dried apricots
6 ounces pitted prunes
1 tablespoon cherry brandy

Drain the cherries thoroughly, reserving the liquid. Combine the brown sugar and cornstarch in a medium mixing bowl. Stir in the cherry juice, lemon juice and orange juice gradually. Combine the cherries, peaches, apricots and prunes in a 2-quart casserole dish. Pour the brown sugar and juice mixture over the fruit. Sprinkle with the brandy. Cover and bake at 350 degrees for 45 minutes or until the apricots are tender. Serve warm.

Makes twelve 2/3-cup servings.

This is a wonderful winter-time side dish.

Apple Dumplings

2 tart apples, peeled and sliced
Two 8-ounce cans crescent rolls
2 sticks margarine, melted
1/2 cup sugar
1 teaspoon cinnamon
12 ounces clear soft drink

Cut the apples into 8 slices each. Wrap each slice with a crescent roll, sealing the edges. Place in a baking dish. Combine the margarine, sugar and cinnamon. Sprinkle over the rolls. Pour the soft drink over the rolls. Bake at 350 degrees 25 to 30 minutes or until golden brown.

We serve these dumplings at breakfast or as a dessert with a scoop of vanilla ice cream.

Tempting Cheese Crêpes

3/4 cup all-purpose flour
1/2 teaspoon salt
3 eggs, beaten
1 cup milk
Two 8-ounce packages cream cheese, softened
1/4 cup sugar
1 teaspoon vanilla extract
10-ounce package frozen strawberries, thawed, drained, reserving liquid
1 tablespoon cornstarch
1 banana, sliced

Combine the flour, salt and eggs in a mixing bowl. Stir in the milk. Pour 1/2 cup of the mixture into a hot, lightly coated 8-inch skillet. Cook over a medium-high heat until lightly brown, turning once. Remove from the skillet. Combine the cream cheese, sugar and vanilla. Mix well and spread 1/4 cup on each crêpe. Fold into thirds and place in a 9x13-inch baking dish. Refrigerate, if desired. Bake at 350 degrees for 15 to 20 minutes or until thoroughly heated. Combine the liquid from the strawberries with water to make 1 1/4 cups. Add the cornstarch gradually. Stir until blended. Bring to a boil, stirring constantly. Boil 1 minute. Stir in the strawberries and banana. Spoon over crêpes.

Makes 10 to 12 crêpes.

Homestyle Breakfast Casserole

6 eggs
1 pint heavy cream
1 cup shredded Cheddar cheese
1/2 cup cooked, crumbled bacon
1/3 cup sliced mushrooms
1/2 cup frozen hash browns, thawed
1/4 teaspoon salt

Whisk the eggs and cream until frothy. Stir in the cheese until blended. Add the bacon, mushrooms, potatoes and salt. Pour into a coated 9x9x2-inch baking dish. Cover and refrigerate overnight. Bake uncovered at 350 degrees for 40 to 45 minutes or until lightly brown and a knife inserted near the center comes out clean.

Sausage Breakfast Casserole

1 pound sausage, cooked and drained
3 slices bread, cubed
6 eggs
2 cups milk
1 teaspoon dry mustard
Salt and pepper to taste
1 cup grated sharp Cheddar cheese

Spread the sausage in 9x13-inch dish. Sprinkle the cubed bread over the sausage. Beat the eggs, milk, mustard, salt and pepper in a mixing bowl. Pour the egg mixture over the bread. Top with the cheese. Refrigerate overnight. Bake at 350 degrees for 45 minutes.

Easy Breakfast Squares

24 ounces frozen shredded hash browns, thawed
1 1/2 cups shredded mozzarella cheese
1 1/2 cups shredded Cheddar cheese
1 onion, diced
2 cups cooked, chopped ham
Salt and pepper to taste
3 eggs, beaten
1 cup milk

Layer the hash browns, mozzarella cheese, Cheddar cheese, onion, ham, salt and pepper in a lightly coated 9x13-inch baking dish. Set aside. Beat the eggs and milk in a small bowl. Pour over the hash browns. Refrigerate overnight. Bake uncovered at 350 degrees for 45 minutes.

Serves 6 to 8.

The soul needs friendship....the heart needs Love.

Herb Tarts

Savory Herb Tart

2 cups flour
Pinch of salt
1/2 cup cold butter
1 egg yolk
1 teaspoon lemon juice
2 tablespoon cold water
3/4 cup grated sharp Cheddar cheese
1 egg
1/2 cup milk
Salt and pepper to taste
Finely chopped oregano and basil, fresh or dried
Fresh parsley, chopped

Sift the flour and salt into a medium-size bowl. Cut in the butter with a pastry blender until the mixture resembles coarse crumbs. Stir the egg yolk and lemon juice in a small bowl. Pour into the flour mixture and add enough cold water until the dough is the consistency needed. Turn the dough onto a floured surface and knead lightly. Wrap in waxed paper and refrigerate for 30 minutes. Coat a 2-inch tartlet pan. Roll out the pastry on a floured surface. Cut out 12 rounds with a 2 1/2-inch cookie cutter. Line each cup of the tartlet with a pastry round. Sprinkle each with one tablespoon cheese. Whisk the egg, milk, salt, pepper and herbs. Pour into the pastry shells and sprinkle with chopped parsley. Bake at 350 degrees for 35 to 40 minutes until the pastry is golden and filling is set. Serve warm.

For country ham tarts, add 1 tablespoon minced country ham to each tart. For bacon tarts, add 1 tablespoon bacon bits to each tart.

Prepackaged tart shells can be used when in a hurry.

Makes 12 tarts.

Egg Hamlette

8 slices ham, cut into round shape
2 cups grated cheese
1/3 cup milk
1 egg
1/2 teaspoon oregano
1/2 teaspoon basil

Place two slices of the ham into each coated muffin tin. Add 1/4 cup of cheese. Combine the remaining ingredients in a mixing bowl. Pour over the cheese and ham. Bake at 350 degrees for 20 minutes.

Makes 4 servings.

This is my husband, Richard's favorite dish to make for Bennett House guests. Especially if he only has one or two people. It is easy, no left-overs, and quick clean-up if you use the new silicone muffin pans.

Glazed Bacon

1/2 cup flour
1/3 cup brown sugar
1 teaspoon freshly-ground black pepper
1 teaspoon cinnamon, optional
1 pound bacon, thickly sliced

Combine the flour, brown sugar, pepper and cinnamon in a gallon-size plastic bag. Place one piece of bacon at a time in the bag and shake well to coat. Line a cookie sheet with parchment paper. Place the bacon on the cookie sheet so slices are not touching one another. Bake at 300 degrees for 30 to 40 minutes. Drain on paper towels.

Salmon and Cheddar Strata

6 eggs
1 pint heavy cream
1 cup shredded Cheddar cheese
1/4 teaspoon salt
14 3/4-ounce can pink salmon, drained and flaked

Whisk the eggs with the cream in a mixing bowl until frothy. Stir in the cheese. Add the salt and fold in the salmon. Pour into a buttered casserole dish and refrigerate overnight. Bake at 350 degrees for 40 minutes or until a knife inserted in the center comes out clean. Serve with fresh fruit, southern biscuits and slightly frozen tomato juice.

Colorful Ham Omelet

3 tablespoons butter or margarine
1/4 cup finely chopped onion
1/4 cup finely chopped green pepper
1/2 cup chopped ham
6 eggs, lightly beaten
1/4 cup shredded Cheddar cheese

Melt 1 tablespoon of the butter in a small skillet over a medium heat. Add the onions and green peppers. Sauté 3 to 5 minutes or until tender. Add the ham; heat thoroughly. Remove from the skillet and set aside. Melt 1 tablespoon of the butter in the same skillet over a medium heat; add 3 well-beaten eggs. Cook the eggs, pulling the edges toward the center until almost set. Spoon half of the ham mixture over the eggs. Cook until set. Fold in half. Repeat with the remaining eggs and ham mixture. Sprinkle with cheese and serve.

Makes 2 omelets.

tea sandwiches, soups & salads

Little girls throughout the ages have grown up having tea parties. The Bennett House provided memories from the first Bennett ladies that lived here -- Belle, Sue, Sally, Elizabeth and Helen to the many little girls, mothers, and grandmothers that continue to come even now. When the teapot is boiling and the tarts are baking, we know memories are about to be made.

Photo courtesy of Eastern Kentucky University Archives, Richmond, Kentucky

Double-Filled Tea Sandwiches

Cheese-and-Orange Filling

11-ounce can mandarin oranges, drained
8-ounce package cream cheese, softened
1/2 cup finely chopped walnuts, toasted
1/2 teaspoon ground cinnamon

Press the orange segments between paper towels to remove the excess moisture. Combine the oranges and the remaining ingredients in a food processor. Pulse until smooth and blended.

Tomato-Curry-Orange Filling

1/2 cup butter or margarine, softened
1/4 teaspoon curry powder
1/4 teaspoon grated orange rind
1/4 teaspoon ketchup
1/8 teaspoon salt

Combine all the ingredients in a small bowl. Mix well.

18 slices oatmeal bread
Cheese-and-Orange Filling
Tomato-Curry-Orange Filling
Orange strip and leaves for garnish

Remove the crust from the bread. Spread half of the bread slices with Cheese-and-Orange Filling; spread the remaining bread slices with Tomato-Curry-Orange Filling. Place the different fillings together. Cut into quarters. Garnish with orange strip and leaves. To make one day ahead, cover the top of the prepared sandwiches with wax paper. Top with slightly dampened white paper towel and store in the refrigerator.

Makes 36 tea sandwiches.

Goldenrod Tea Sandwiches

Pimento Cheese Filling

1/2 pound grated sharp Cheddar cheese
1/2 pound processed American cheese
1/4 cup mayonnaise
5 tablespoons sweet pickle juice
2 dashes of cayenne pepper

Mix the ingredients in a food processor until blended. Mixture should be slightly lumpy. Refrigerate.

Apricot Filling

1 cup dried apricots
2 cups water
1/2 cup sugar
8-ounce package cream cheese, softened
Dash of salt
Loaf of wheat sandwich bread
Loaf of white sandwich bread

Add the water to the apricots in a saucepan and cook over a medium heat until softened. Add the sugar and continue to cook until some of the apricots begin to dissolve. Cool. Process the cream cheese, apricots and salt in a food processor. Spread one slice of the wheat bread with the Pimento Cheese Filling; spread another slice of the wheat bread with the Apricot Filling. Place a white slice of bread between the two slices of covered wheat bread. Cut into strips for ribbon sandwiches.

Chicken and Olive Tea Sandwiches

1 cup cooked, diced chicken
1/2 cup stuffed green olives, drained and thinly sliced
1/3 cup pimientos, drained and chopped
4 medium green onions, finely chopped
Sour cream to moisten
1 loaf sandwich bread, frozen and cut into 2-inch rounds
Olive slices for garnish

Combine the chicken, olives, pimientos and onions in a medium mixing bowl. Moisten with the sour cream until spreadable. Spread over the bread. Garnish with the olive slices. Place in an airtight container with a moist white paper towel.

Apple Cinnamon Spread on Raisin Bread

Two 8-ounce packages cream cheese, softened
1/2 cup raisins
1/4 cup orange marmalade
1/2 teaspoon cinnamon
Dash of nutmeg
1 apple, diced
1 loaf raisin bread
Lettuce, optional

Combine the cream cheese, raisins, marmalade, cinnamon, nutmeg and apple in a large bowl. Spread onto the raisin bread. Add lettuce if desired.

Cran-Turkey Sandwiches

.04-ounce package cranberry orange sauce
2 tablespoons Dijon mustard
1 loaf whole wheat bread
1/4 pound sliced turkey
Lettuce

Combine the cranberry sauce and mustard in a small bowl. Spread on a slice of bread. Top with the sliced turkey and lettuce.

May Day Tea Sandwiches

4 large hard-cooked eggs, peeled and finely chopped
1/4 cup mayonnaise or as needed to mix
1 teaspoon Dijon mustard
2 teaspoons chopped fresh tarragon
2 teaspoons chopped fresh chives
2 teaspoons red pepper and artichoke tapenade
1/2 teaspoon fresh lemon zest
Salt and pepper to taste
Dash of lemon juice or bottled hot sauce
16 slices fine-textured white or wheat bread or oatmeal bread
Butter, softened
Black olives, pickled red peppers or alfalfa sprouts for garnish

Combine the eggs, mayonnaise, mustard, tarragon, chives, tapenade and zest in a large bowl. Mix well. Season to taste with salt, pepper, lemon juice or hot sauce. Spread each slice of the bread with butter. Spread with the egg mixture. Top with a bread slice. Cut off the crust and cut into finger sandwiches or rounds. Garnish.

Vegetable Spread for Sandwiches

Two 8-ounce packages cream cheese, softened
3/4 cup sour cream
2 tablespoons flour
4 eggs
2 garlic cloves, minced
2 tablespoons lemon juice
1 teaspoon salt
1 teaspoon chili powder
1/2 teaspoon pepper
1/4 teaspoon paprika
1/4 teaspoon hot sauce
1 cup shredded Cheddar cheese
1/2 cup finely chopped carrots
1/4 cup finely chopped broccoli
1/4 cup finely chopped green onions
1 loaf party rye
1 cup chopped tomatoes
2 tablespoons chopped fresh parsley
2 tablespoons chopped fresh chives

Combine the cream cheese, sour cream and flour in a mixing bowl. Beat until well blended. Add the eggs, one at a time, beating well after each addition. Add the garlic, lemon juice, salt, chili powder, pepper, paprika and hot sauce. Mix well. Fold in the Cheddar cheese, carrots, broccoli and green onions. Spoon the vegetable mixture into a coated 9-inch springform pan. Bake at 375 degrees for 35 to 45 minutes or until set. Cool in the pan. Remove the side of the pan. Cover and chill in the refrigerator until ready to use. Cut each piece of the party rye in half diagonally. Spread about a tablespoon of paté on top and garnish with tomatoes, parsley and chives.

Makes 45 small sandwiches.

Celebration Sandwiches

12 ounces water-packed flake tuna, drained
2 tablespoons mayonnaise
4 teaspoons finely diced green pepper
4 teaspoons finely diced red bell pepper
2 tablespoons finely diced red onion
1/2 teaspoon chopped fresh parsley
1 teaspoon rice wine vinegar
1/2 teaspoon lemon juice
7 drops hot pepper sauce
Salt and pepper to taste
1 loaf fine-textured white or wheat bread
Butter, softened

Combine the ingredients except the bread and butter in a large bowl. Mix well. Refrigerate one hour. Spread each slice of the bread with butter. Spread half the slices with the tuna mixture and top with the remaining slices. Cut off the crusts. Cut each sandwich into 3 to 4 finger sandwiches. Wrap tightly in plastic wrap or cover with a damp tea towel until ready to serve.

Ham-Pineapple Tea Sandwiches with Honey Butter

1 cup minced ham
1/2 cup crushed pineapple, drained
1 teaspoon Dijon mustard
Pepper to taste
2 tablespoons honey
2 sticks butter, softened
20 thin slices whole wheat bread

Combine the ham, pineapple, mustard and pepper in a medium bowl. Set aside. Blend the honey and butter in a small bowl. Spread the honey butter on all the bread slices. Top half the slices with the ham mixture. Top with the remaining slices. Remove the crusts. Cut each sandwich into four triangles.

Makes 40 finger sandwiches.

Cucumber Tea Sandwiches

1 large cucumber, peeled, seeded and grated
8-ounce package cream cheese, softened
1 tablespoon mayonnaise
1 small shallot, minced
1/4 teaspoon seasoned salt
1 loaf sandwich bread, frozen
Butter, softened
Cucumber slices for garnish

Drain the cucumber well, pressing between layers of paper towels. Stir the cucumber, cream cheese, mayonnaise, shallot and salt in a mixing bowl. Butter the slices of bread. Spread the cucumber mixture evenly over half of the slices. Top with the remaining slices. Cut off the crusts. Cut into triangles. Garnish if desired. Store in an airtight container.

Egg Salad and Pimiento Cheese Stack

12 eggs, hard boiled
1 bunch green onions
3 tablespoons sweet pickle relish
Salt and pepper to taste
Mayonnaise
4 cups grated cheese
4-ounce jar pimientos, chopped
1 cup almonds, toasted
1 loaf white bread
1 loaf wheat bread

Chop the eggs and green onions. Combine the eggs, onions, pickle relish, salt and pepper in a mixing bowl. Add enough of the mayonnaise to create a spreadable consistency. Refrigerate. Pulse the cheese, pimientos, almonds and pepper in a food processor. Add enough of the mayonnaise to create a spreadable consistency. Spread the egg mixture on the white bread slices and the pimiento mixture on the wheat slices. Sandwich together and cut into four squares.

Makes 50 tea sandwiches.

Olive Nut Tea Sandwiches

1 loaf white sandwich bread
8-ounce package cream cheese, softened
1/4 cup chopped walnuts
1/4 cup chopped olives
1 tablespoon mayonnaise
Pimientos, sliced olives and parsley for garnish

Remove the crusts from the bread and cut into desired shapes. Blend the cream cheese, walnuts, olives and mayonnaise in a food processor. Spread the mixture evenly over each cut out of bread. Garnish with pimientos, olives and parsley.

Makes 32 open-faced sandwiches.

Tea Plate with Olive Nut Tea Sandwich

Benedictine Tea Sandwiches

2 medium cucumbers, peeled, seeded and grated
12 ounces cream cheese, softened
1 small onion, grated
Salt to taste
Green food coloring
Mayonnaise
1 loaf bread, crust removed
Thinly sliced cucumbers or parsley for garnish

Combine the cucumbers and cream cheese in a food processor. Blend in the onion and salt. Stir in enough of the mayonnaise to make the mixture spreadable. Add enough green food coloring to make the spread a pale green. Spread evenly over the slices of bread. Garnish with cucumbers or parsley.

Makes 45 open-faced sandwiches.

Valentine Tea Party Sandwiches

1 pound baked ham
1/4 cup celery
1/4 cup green onions
2 tablespoons mayonnaise
1 loaf white or wheat sandwich bread, cut into 2-inch rounds
1 cup orange marmalade
15-ounce can sliced beets

Chop the ham, celery and green onions in a food processor. Add the mayonnaise to blend the mixture and make it spreadable. Refrigerate until ready to use. Spread half of the bread with the ham mixture and half with the orange marmalade. Place the ham mixture slices on top of the marmalade slices. Drain the beets and pat dry. Cut a small heart from each beet slice with a heart-shaped cookie cutter. Place on top of each sandwich.

3-tiered tea tray

South-of-the-Border Black Bean Soup

15-ounce can black beans, rinsed and drained
14 1/2-ounce can no-salt added whole tomatoes, chopped
14 1/2-ounce can diced tomatoes with green chiles
14 1/2-ounce can chicken broth
4-ounce can whole green chiles, drained and coarsely chopped
1 1/2 cups frozen corn
4 green onions, thinly sliced
3 tablespoons chili powder
2 teaspoons cumin
1 teaspoon dried minced garlic
Light or no-fat sour cream, Colby-jack reduced fat shredded cheese, tortilla chips and green onions for garnish

Place all the soup ingredients in a slow cooker. Cover and cook on a low setting 7 to 9 hours. Ladle into bowls. Top with 1 tablespoons sour cream, 1 tablespoon shredded cheese, 4 crushed chips and green onions.

Makes 8 to 10 servings.

Bean Soup

3/4 cup chopped onion
1/2 cup chopped green pepper
1 clove garlic, minced
2 tablespoons margarine
Two 15-ounce cans Great Northern beans, undrained
16-ounce can chopped tomatoes
2 cups water
1 teaspoon salt
1/8 teaspoon pepper
6 frankfurters or smoked sausage, sliced

Sauté the onion, green pepper, garlic and margarine in a heavy saucepan until tender but not brown. Add the beans, tomatoes, water, salt and pepper. Bring to a boil. Reduce the heat. Cover and simmer 10 to 15 minutes. Add the frankfurters or sausage. Cover and cook 5 to 10 minutes more.

White Chili Chicken Soup

1 tablespoon butter or margarine, melted
4 cups cooked, chopped chicken
1 large onion, chopped
3 carrots, chopped
2 garlic cloves, minced
Two 14-ounce cans chicken broth
1 tablespoon chicken bouillon granules
1 teaspoon ground cumin
1/4 teaspoon ground red pepper
Three 15-ounce cans Great Northern beans, 1 can mashed
4 1/4-ounce can green chiles, chopped
2 tablespoons all-purpose flour
1/2 cup milk
1/4 cup chopped fresh cilantro
Cheddar cheese, sour cream, green onions and crumbled bacon for garnish

Combine the butter, chicken, onion, carrots and garlic in a large pan. Sauté for 10 minutes. Add the chicken broth, bouillon, cumin, red pepper, 2 cans of the beans and green chiles. Bring to a boil and simmer 20 minutes. Combine the flour and milk in a small bowl. Add to the soup with the cilantro and 1 can mashed beans. Cook until thickened. Serve with the garnish of your choice.

Makes 12 cups.

Potato Soup

6 potatoes, peeled and cut into bite-size pieces
1 onion, finely chopped
1 carrot, pared and sliced
1 stalk celery, sliced
4 chicken bouillon cubes
1 tablespoon parsley flakes
5 cups water
1 teaspoon salt
2 tablespoons butter
Pepper to taste
13-ounce can evaporated milk
1/2 cup instant potato flakes
Chopped chives for garnish

Combine all the ingredients except the evaporated milk, potato flakes and chives in a large pot. Bring to a boil, reduce heat and simmer at least until the vegetables are tender, about 1 1/2 hours. Stir in the evaporated milk during the last half hour. Mash the vegetables with a masher before adding the milk if desired. Stir in the potato flakes. Top with the chives and serve. If using a crock-pot, cook 10 to 12 hours on low or 3 to 4 hours on high.

Hot Brown Soup

1/4 cup minced onion
1/4 cup butter, melted
1/4 cup all-purpose flour
1/2 teaspoon garlic salt
1/8 teaspoon hot sauce
4 cups milk
1 cup shredded Cheddar cheese
1/2 cup cooked, chopped country or city ham
1/2 cup cooked, chopped turkey
Bacon, tomatoes and chopped parsley for garnish

Sauté the onions in the butter until tender. Add the flour, garlic salt and hot sauce. Stir 1 minute. Add the milk and cook until thick. Reduce the heat and add the cheese. Stir in the ham and turkey. Do not boil. Ladle into bowls. Garnish and serve.

Jessica Parker's Taco Soup

1 1/2 pounds lean ground beef (sirloin is best)
1 large onion
1 clove garlic, minced
1 1/2-ounce package taco seasoning mix
28-ounce can diced tomatoes
Two 16-ounce cans kidney beans, drained
28-ounce can tomato sauce
10 1/2-ounce can beef broth
Two 4 1/2-ounce cans chopped green chilies
3 tablespoons jalapeno pepper or pepper relish
1/2 cup water
1 teaspoon chili powder
1 teaspoon cumin
Finely shredded iceberg lettuce, shredded Cheddar cheese, chopped tomato, corn chips or oven baked tortilla chips and sour cream for garnish

Brown the beef, onion and garlic in Dutch oven and drain. Add the taco seasoning and stir well. Add the tomatoes, beans, tomato sauce, broth, chilies, peppers and water and stir well. Add the chili powder and cumin. Bring to a boil. Cover, reduce the heat and simmer for 30 minutes. Ladle into soup bowls and garnish as desired.

County Extension Agents often wear many hats. I wrote a weekly newspaper column in the Richmond Register *for over 25 years. Often my deadline would be near and I would send a call to the readers to help out. Jessica Parker gave me this recipe one cold January and it became a staple for tailgating and Superbowl parties.*

Oriental Pasta Salad

8 ounces linguini or fettuccini, broken into thirds
4 green onions,sliced
2 carrots, scraped and thinly sliced
12 cherry tomatoes, halved
1 pound fresh broccoli, thinly sliced
1/2 cup vegetable oil
1/2 cup soy sauce
1 clove garlic, minced
1/4 cup lemon juice
1/4 teaspoon hot sauce
2 tablespoons sesame seeds

Cook the linguine according to the package directions; drain. Rinse with cold water and drain. Add the green onion, carrots, tomatoes and broccoli and toss well.

Combine the oil, soy sauce, garlic, lemon juice, hot sauce and sesame seeds in a jar, cover tightly, and shake vigorously. Pour the dressing, toss gently and serve immediately.

I like to chill this overnight. You can also serve it as a main dish by adding grilled salmon or chicken breast on top.

Asian Cabbage Salad

1/2 head cabbage, thinly sliced
2 green onions, chopped
Juice of one lemon
2 tablespoons sesame seeds, toasted
2 tablespoons slivered almonds, toasted
1 chicken breast, cooked and diced
2 tablespoons sugar
1/2 cup oil
1 teaspoon salt
1/2 teaspoon pepper
3 tablespoons rice vinegar
1 season packet from ramen noodles
3-ounce package ramen noodles, uncooked and broken apart

Combine the cabbage, onion, lemon juice, sesame seeds and almonds in a large salad bowl. Add the chicken on top of the cabbage mixture. Combine the sugar, oil, salt, pepper, vinegar and season packet to make dressing. Add the noodles and dressing to the salad just before serving. Toss to coat.

Makes 6 servings.

Granny Courtney's Fruit Salad

2 medium apples, chopped
2 oranges, peeled and chopped
1 cup chopped grapes
20-ounce can pineapple chunks, drained, reserving juice
1 to 2 bananas, peeled and cut in equal rounds
1/2 cup sugar
2 tablespoons all-purpose flour
1 egg, beaten

Toss the apples, oranges, grapes, pineapple and bananas in a large bowl; set aside. Combine the pineapple juice, sugar, flour and egg in a glass mixing bowl. Microwave on high for 2 minutes. Stir thoroughly. Microwave 1 minute more or until the mixture starts to thicken. Stir until smooth. Cool and toss over the fruit. Store in the refrigerator. If making ahead of time, add the bananas when ready to serve.

Makes 6 to 8 servings.

This is a wonderful wintertime fruit salad. The cooked dressing gives it a special taste. It is a great side dish for the holiday meals or special events such as showers and receptions. Serve it in a crystal compote for large groups.

Mrs. Miller's Salad

21-ounce can cherry pie filling
20-ounce can crushed pineapple, drained
14-ounce can sweetened condensed milk
16-ounce container nondairy topping
1 cup chopped nuts
1 cup coconut

Combine all the ingredients in a large mixing bowl. Spread into a 9x13-inch pan, cupcake papers or tin can. Freeze.

Makes 30 cupcake-size servings.

Mrs. Millers Salad

Broccoli Salad

1 head fresh broccoli, chopped into bite-size pieces
1 cup sunflower seeds
1/2 small onion, chopped
1/2 cup raisins
1/2 pound bacon, cooked and crumbled
1 cup mayonnaise
1/2 cup sugar
2 tablespoons vinegar

Combine the broccoli, sunflower seeds, onion, raisins and bacon in a large bowl. Combine the mayonnaise, sugar and vinegar in a small bowl. Mix well. Pour over the salad just before serving.

Cranberry Salad

12-ounce package fresh cranberries
1 cup cold water
1 cup sugar
3-ounce package strawberry gelatin
1 cup boiling water
1 cup cold water
5 1/2-ounce can crushed pineapple, drained
2 cups chopped apples
1 cup chopped celery
1 cup chopped pecans

Cook the cranberries in the water in a saucepan until the cranberries begin to pop and are soft. Add the sugar and cook for 15 minutes. Cool slightly. Stir the strawberry gelatin into 1 cup of boiling water in a large bowl until dissolved. Add 1 cup of cold water. Add the pineapple, apples, celery, pecans and cranberries. Mix well. Pour into a coated 9x13-inch glass dish. Refrigerate overnight until ready to serve. Cut into 2-inch squares and serve on a lettuce leaf.

Makes 12 servings.

Bennett House Signature Salad

1 head bibb lettuce, torn into pieces
1 large head romaine lettuce, torn into pieces
Two 11-ounce cans mandarin orange slices, drained or 1 cup fresh strawberries, sliced
1/4 cup slivered almonds, toasted
1/2 cup chopped red onion
Strawberry Dressing

Combine the lettuces, orange slices or strawberries, almonds and onion in a large salad bowl. Toss with Strawberry Dressing.

Makes 10 to 12 servings.

Strawberry Dressing

16-ounce package frozen strawberries, thawed
1 1/2 teaspoons honey
1/4 teaspoon dried thyme
1/4 teaspoon pepper
3 tablespoons raspberry vinegar
1/2 cup water
2 teaspoons oil
1 teaspoon soy sauce

Combine all the ingredients in a blender or food processor and purée until thoroughly blended. Pour the dressing into a covered container and refrigerate. Serve over Bennett House Signature Salad.

Makes 2 cups.

Apricot Salad

Two 3-ounce packages apricot gelatin
2 cups boiling water
2 cups cold water
20-ounce can crushed pineapple, drained, reserving juice
4-ounce jar baby food apricots
3 bananas, diced
1/2 cup sugar
2 tablespoons all-purpose flour
2 tablespoons butter
1 egg, beaten
1 cup pineapple juice
8-ounce package cream cheese
8-ounce container nondairy whipped topping

Dissolve the gelatin in boiling water in a large mixing bowl. Add the cold water and refrigerate until the gelatin is partially set. Add the pineapple, apricots and bananas. Refrigerate until firmly jelled. Combine the sugar, flour, butter, egg and pineapple juice in a saucepan. Cook until thick. Add the cream cheese. Mix well. Cool. Add the whipped topping. Spread on top of the apricot gelatin.

The Bennett House monthly teas are a work of art. Stimulating the senses through the many details of these productions makes the work fun. The more senses I can involve, the better. From the containers selected for the fresh flower arrangement to the china for each table, I deliberately try to awaken the five senses to enrich the activity and make the time spent doing it more enjoyable.

Marinated Vegetable Salad

15-ounce can English peas, drained
11-ounce can white Shoe Peg corn
15 1/2-ounce can French-style green beans, drained
2-ounce jar diced pimentos, drained
1/2 cup diced celery
1/2 cup sugar
1/2 cup chopped onion
1/2 teaspoon pepper
1/2 cup chopped green pepper
1 teaspoon salt
1/2 cup oil
3/4 cup vinegar

Lightly combine the peas, corn, green beans, pimentos and celery in a large mixing bowl. Set aside. Combine the remaining ingredients in a medium saucepan or glass dish. Bring to a boil over low heat or cook in a microwave for 2 minutes. Cool slightly. Pour over the vegetables. Gently toss to coat. Cover and chill 24 hours. Drain and serve.

Makes 6 to 8 servings.

This recipe is a favorite of my son-in-law, Miles Penn, who is also a good cook. Use this any season; it is especially colorful for the holidays.

Macaroni Salad

5 quarts water
1 tablespoon salt
1 pound medium-size shell macaroni
2 carrots, shredded
1 medium onion, finely chopped
1 1/2 cups mayonnaise
Salt and pepper to taste

Bring the water to a rapid boil in a large pan. Add the salt and macaroni. Cook uncovered until tender, about 10 minutes. Drain off the water. Add the carrots, onion, mayonnaise, salt and pepper. Toss lightly. Cool. Refrigerate until ready to serve. Add more mayonnaise if needed.

Our family has the strangest story about macaroni and cheese. Actually, it is a mock macaroni and cheese. About 50 years ago, my mother, Margaret Reynolds Hunter, got this recipe from her cousin, Anna Elizabeth King. She brought it to a family reunion and everyone loved it. Through the years, it has become my mother's trademark. She brings it to every reunion, every big family potluck and every family holiday get-together. As my girls were growing up, they loved it and we always brought the leftovers home with us (it is actually better the second or third day). Now that my daughters are married, their husbands surprisingly love the dish and now the guys ask for the leftovers. My youngest daughter, Ashley, recently married Matt Tabb and he loves this dish. We tease him during the family meals that we are going to eat it all and he won't have any to take home with him. (They even bring their own take-home containers so they are sure to get some of the leftovers.) We call it mock macaroni and cheese because it does not have any cheese but rather shredded carrots that look like cheese. This recipe makes a large amount and keeps well in the refrigerator. I think that is why my mother always made it. She could serve it with any type of meat or I remember just eating a bowl the next day for lunch. It's so basic, very few ingredients, and looks very plain, but it tastes so good. I can't explain it.

Pretzel Salad

1 cup crushed pretzels
3 tablespoons sugar
1 cup chopped pecans
1 stick margarine, melted
8-ounce package cream cheese
8-ounce container nondairy whipped topping, thawed
1 cup powdered sugar
5.1-ounce box strawberry gelatin
2 cups boiling water
16-ounce package frozen strawberries, thawed

Combine the pretzels, sugar, pecans and margarine. Press into the bottom of a 9x13-inch dish. Bake at 350 degrees for 8 to 10 minutes. Beat the cream cheese, whipped topping and powdered sugar until smooth. Spread on top of the pretzel mixture. Place in the refrigerator for 30 minutes. Dissolve the gelatin in boiling water. Add the strawberries. Stir until the gelatin begins to thicken. Pour over the cream cheese mixture and refrigerate overnight. Cut into squares to serve.

Some say this salad is good enough to be a dessert!

Broccoli Slaw with Cranberries

12-ounce package broccoli slaw mix
2 sweet apples, chopped
1 cup dried cranberries
1/2 cup apple cider vinegar
3/4 cup sugar
1/2 teaspoon salt
1/2 teaspoon mustard seeds
3 tablespoons oil

Combine the slaw mix, apples and cranberries in a mixing bowl. Set aside. Combine the vinegar, sugar, salt and mustard seeds in a glass bowl. Microwave for 2 minutes. Whisk in the oil. Pour over the slaw. Cover and chill.

Makes 8 servings.

Oriental Slaw

16-ounce package coleslaw
1 to 2 bunches green onions, sliced
1 cup sunflower seeds
1 cup sliced almonds
3-ounce package oriental-flavored ramen noodles, crumbled
1/3 cup sugar
3/4 cup oil
1/4 cup white wine vinegar
Seasoning packet from ramen noodles

Mix the coleslaw, green onions, sunflower seeds, almonds and noodles in a medium bowl. Set aside. Combine the sugar, oil, vinegar and seasoning packet in a small bowl. Pour over the slaw just prior to serving. Toss to coat. Do not let the slaw sit in the dressing too long before serving.

Jellied Cranberry-Orange Relish

4 cups cranberries, fresh or frozen
2 oranges
2 cups sugar
Two 3-ounce packages lemon gelatin
2 cups boiling water
3/4 cup cold water

Put the cranberries through a food chopper or processor. Quarter the oranges, remove the seeds and put through a food chopper, including the peeling. Blend the cranberries, oranges and sugar in a large bowl. Dissolve the gelatin in the boiling water in a medium bowl. Add the cold water. Chill until slightly thickened. Add to the cranberry mixture. Mix well. Transfer to a coated mold. Chill until firm. Unmold into a serving plate.

The inspiration for little girls dress-up tea parties came from the tea parties I had with my grandmother, Lucille Reynolds Courtney, many years ago. I still remember her collection of teacups and saucers, which were displayed in the window shelves in her sun porch room. Now, I have many of those cups and saucers on the mantel in the Belle Room at the Bennett House. I find that our guests just love to sit in front of the fireplace and view the different tea cup handles, style and color combinations. I tell them tea cups are like people, each one different, unique and special in their own way.

Vegetables in Aspic Jelly

1 1/3 tablespoons plain gelatin
2/3 cup cold chicken broth
2 cups tomato juice
1/4 cup lemon juice
2/3 teaspoon salt
1/4 teaspoon pepper
2 tablespoons sugar
2/3 cup green beans, cooked
2/3 cup grated cauliflower
1/3 cup chopped green pepper
1/4 cup finely chopped green onions
2/3 cup grated cabbage
1/4 cup peeled, chopped cucumbers
2/3 cup chopped pecans

Sprinkle the gelatin over the chicken broth in a large bowl and let stand 10 minutes. Bring the tomato juice to a boil in a saucepan. Add to the broth. Add the lemon juice, salt, pepper and sugar and mix well. Refrigerate until it begins to congeal. Fold in the vegetables and nuts. Spoon into a coated mold or pan. Refrigerate until set. Serve with Whipped Cream Dressing.

Whipped Cream Dressing

2 cups whipped cream
1 cup mayonnaise

Combine the whipped cream and mayonnaise in a small bowl. Mix well.

Ambrosia Laced Peaches

1 1/2 cups seedless green grapes, halved
Three 15 1/2-ounce cans pineapple tidbits, drained
1 1/2 cups orange sections
1 1/2 cups flaked coconut
1 1/2 cups sour cream
40 peach halves, drained
40 lettuce leaves
1 1/2 cups slivered almonds, toasted

Combine the grapes, pineapple, oranges and coconut in a large mixing bowl. Toss gently and chill. Before serving, add the sour cream. Mix well. Place each peach half on a lettuce leaf and fill with 1/4 cup fruit mixture. Top with the almonds.

Makes 40 servings.

This recipe serves a crowd! Adjust accordingly for your family. It is a great way to get your fruit requirements for the day.

Bennett House Chicken Salad

4 cups finely chopped cooked chicken
1 cup finely chopped celery
1 cup halved red grapes
1 cup finely chopped sweet pickles
1 cup finely chopped pecans
1 1/2 to 2 cups mayonnaise
Red grapes, cut in half for garnish

Combine the chicken, celery, grapes, pickles and pecans in a bowl. Add the mayonnaise and mix until well blended. Add more mayonnaise if it seems dry. Spoon into miniature phyllo shells and garnish with grape halve.

Cream Cheese Tart Shells

3-ounce package cream cheese
1/2 cup soft butter
1 cup sifted flour

Blend the cream cheese and butter until smooth in a small bowl. Add the flour until well blended. Chill at least 2 hours. Shape into 24 one-inch balls. Press into coated miniature muffin tins. Bake at 375 for 15 to 20 minutes. Cool. Fill with Bennett House Chicken Salad just before serving.

This is my mother, Margaret Hunter's, recipe. She claims the reason it is so good is she hand chops each ingredient. It takes longer, but really does make a difference.

We are always cooking for large groups at the Bennett House. But if you're in a hurry, use cooked chicken from the deli salad bar.

I prefer to served the chicken salad in cream cheese tart shells. They take longer to make but again, it's really worth the effort.

We serve this every month at tea.

entrées

Country-Style Pork Ribs

4 pounds country-style pork ribs
Salt and seasoned pepper to taste
4-ounce jar baby food peaches or 1 cup puréed canned peaches
1/2 cup chili sauce or ketchup
1/2 cup apple cider vinegar
3 tablespoons soy sauce
1/4 cup brown sugar
3 cloves garlic, crushed
1 tablespoon ground ginger

Rub the ribs on all sides with the salt and pepper. Place the ribs meaty side down in a foil-lined pan. Bake at 450 degrees for 20 minutes. Spoon off the excess fat. Blend the remaining ingredients and pour over the ribs. Cover and reduce the oven temperature to 350 degrees. Bake 1 1/2 hours or until tender. Remove the cover 20 minutes before the ribs are done so meat can brown. Baste with the sauce several times while browning.

Makes 8 servings.

Former Madison County 4-H Extension Agent, Jo Nelda Cole, served this when we visited her family at Dale Hollow Lake. Maybe it was the long day on the water, but food always tastes better when you're on vacation. Serve it with a big bowl of mashed potatoes and folks will like it any time.

Pork Loin Roast with Bourbon Glaze

2 to 2 1/2 pounds boneless pork loin
Salt and pepper to taste
10-ounce jar
Kentucky Bourbon Peach Butter*

Place the pork in a 9x13-inch baking dish. Rub with the salt and pepper. Spoon or brush the peach butter over the pork. Bake uncovered at 350 degrees for 1 hour or until a meat thermometer inserted into the thickest portion registers 160 degrees. Let stand before slicing.

Makes 6 servings.

*You can make your own peach butter by adding 1 to 2 tablespoons Kentucky bourbon to a 18-ounce jar of peach preserves. Stir well and let set overnight.

I found this recipe in the **Pride of Kentucky**, *a collection of recipes published by the Kentucky Association of Family and Consumer Science Extension Agents. It has been a hit every time I serve it.*

Fruit-Stuffed Pork Chops

1/2 cup dried sour cherries
1/2 cup halved, pitted prunes
1/2 cup quartered, dried apricots
1 1/4 cup chicken stock or canned chicken broth
1/2 cup bourbon
4 center-cut pork chops with pocket
2 tablespoons olive oil
1 teaspoon crumbled, dried thyme leaves
Salt and pepper to taste
4 tablespoons unsalted butter

Combine the cherries, prunes, apricots, 3/4 cup broth and bourbon in a medium bowl. Let set 1 hour. Drain the fruit, reserving the liquid. Stuff the pork chops with the fruit mixture, closing with toothpicks. Cook the chops in oil for 5 minutes. Transfer to a roasting pan. Sprinkle with the thyme, salt and pepper. Dot with the butter and add reserved liquid. Bake at 350 degrees for 30 minutes, basting twice. Serve hot.

Cranberry Apricot Pork Tenderloin

1 pound pork tenderloin
3/4 teaspoon salt
1/4 teaspoon ground pepper
1 teaspoon olive oil
1 cup canned cranberry sauce
1/2 cup sliced, dried apricots
1 tablespoon cornstarch
1/2 teaspoon cinnamon
2 teaspoons orange zest

Sprinkle the pork with the salt and pepper. Heat the oil in a large nonstick skillet over a medium heat. Add the pork and cook until browned, turning often. Transfer the pork to a 5 to 6-quart slow cooker. Combine the cranberry sauce, apricots, cornstarch and cinnamon in a medium bowl. Pour over the pork, turning to coat. Cover and cook until the pork is tender, 3 to 4 hours on high or 6 to 8 hours on low. Transfer the pork to a cutting board and cut into 16 slices. Stir the orange zest into the fruit sauce and serve with the pork.

Cook this for dinner while you're shopping, playing or taking a nap! The smell that will fill your home will be a memory maker.

Makes 4 servings.

Cranberry Pecan-Stuffed Pork Chops

2 cups dried cranberries
1 cup orange juice
2 pounds mild pork sausage
4 cups coarsely chopped celery
1 1/2 cups chopped onion
1/2 cup margarine
14-ounce can chicken broth
1 teaspoon salt
1/2 teaspoon pepper
1 teaspoon dried thyme
Two 6-ounce packages pork stuffing mix
2 tablespoons grated orange rind
2 cups chopped pecans
8 to 10 thick pork chops, slit cut for pocket
1/2 cup flour
1 cup cooking wine

Combine the cranberries and orange juice in a small saucepan. Bring to a boil. Remove from the heat and set aside. Brown the sausage in a skillet. Remove the sausage and reserve 2 tablespoons of the drippings in the skillet. Add the celery and onion to the drippings. Cook over a medium heat until transparent. Add the margarine, broth, salt, pepper and thyme. Combine the cranberry mixture, sausage, stuffing mix, onion mixture, orange rind and pecans in a large bowl, stirring until well blended. Spoon 1/2 to 3/4 cup mixture into the pork chop pocket and secure with toothpicks. Roll each chop in the flour and brown in the oil in a skillet. Drain on a paper towel. Transfer the chops to a 9x13-inch baking dish. Add the wine to the skillet and stir over the heat until smooth. Pour the wine sauce over the chops. Cover and bake at 350 degrees for 1 hour. Remove the cover and bake an additional 20 minutes.

Makes 8 to 10 servings.

Men go wild over this.

Ham Balls

1 1/4 pound ground ham
1 pound ground pork
1/2 pound ground beef
1 1/2 cups graham cracker crumbs
2 eggs
1 cup milk
1/4 teaspoon pepper
Two 10 3/4-ounce cans tomato soup
2 cups brown sugar
4 tablespoons vinegar
2 tablespoons dry mustard

Combine the meats, cracker crumbs, eggs, milk and pepper in a large mixing bowl. Shape into balls the size of a large egg. Place in a baking dish. Mix the tomato soup, brown sugar, vinegar and dry mustard in a medium bowl. Pour the sauce over the ham balls. Bake at 350 degrees for 1 hour.

Makes 15 balls.

Pizza Casserole

1 1/2 pounds lean ground beef
1/2 cup chopped onion
1/2 cup chopped bell pepper
1/2 cup sliced mushrooms
1/2 teaspoon salt
Dash of pepper
8 ounces macaroni, cooked
24-ounce can pizza sauce
4 to 6 ounces pepperoni
8 ounces shredded mozzarella cheese
4 ounces shredded Cheddar cheese

Brown the beef, onion, bell pepper and mushrooms over medium heat. Drain. Add the salt, pepper, macaroni and pizza sauce. Stir until blended. Layer half of the macaroni mixture, pepperoni and cheeses in a coated 3-quart casserole dish. Repeat the layers. Bake at 350 degrees for 30 minutes or until hot and the cheese is melted and starts to brown.

This was my daughters, Angela and Ashley's favorite dish as they were growing up. It is a great alternative to pizza. Add a green salad to make a meal.

Dorito Casserole

10 3/4-ounce can cream of mushroom soup
1 cup sour cream
1 small onion, chopped
7-ounce jar salsa
7-ounce package Dorito chips, crushed
3 cups cooked, chopped chicken
2 cups shredded Cheddar cheese

Combine the soup, sour cream, onion and salsa in a large mixing bowl. Layer half of the salsa mixture, chips, chicken and cheese in a casserole dish. Repeat the layers, ending with the cheese. Bake at 400 degrees for 30 minutes.

Barbecued Chicken

2 1/2 pound chicken, quartered or cut up
1/2 cup bottled barbecue sauce
1 tablespoon parsley flakes
1 tablespoon onion flakes

Place the chicken pieces, skin side up, with thick edges toward the outside of a 7x12-inch microwavable baking dish. Combine the barbecue sauce, parsley flakes and onion flakes in a small bowl. Brush 1/2 of the sauce over the top of the chicken. Cover with waxed paper and microwave on high for 10 minutes. Brush with the remaining sauce. Cover and microwave on high for 8 to 10 minutes or until tender. Let stand, covered, for 5 minutes before serving.

Beautiful details abound in the Bennett House. From the cherry wraparound stair case as you enter the foyer to the ornate mantels and original tile fireplaces, every little detail is special. As should be our day to day experiences, for single days experienced fully add up to a lifetime lived deeply and well.

All-American Meat Loaf

1 1/2 pounds lean ground beef
3/4 cup oatmeal
1 medium onion, chopped
1 cup ketchup
1/4 cup milk
2 eggs, beaten
2 tablespoons horseradish
1 1/2 tablespoons salt
1/4 teaspoon pepper
2 tablespoons prepared mustard
1 tablespoons brown sugar

Combine the ground beef, oatmeal, onion, 1/2 cup ketchup, milk, eggs and 1 tablespoon horseradish, salt and pepper in a large mixing bowl and mix well. Spoon into a 10-inch microwavable ring mold or make individual loaves and form a ring on a glass baking dish. Microwave for 12 to 15 minutes. Let stand for 15 minutes. Combine the mustard, remaining horseradish, brown sugar and remaining ketchup; mix well. Invert the ring mold on a glass serving platter or place loaves on a serving dish. Pour the glaze over the meat. Microwave on high for 3 minutes to heat glaze.

Hamburger Corn Bread Casserole

1 pound hamburger
1 medium onion, diced
2 tablespoons Worcestershire sauce
1 1/2 tablespoons chili powder
1 teaspoon salt
1 1/2 cups tomato juice
15 1/2-ounce can kidney beans, drained
1 cup yellow cornmeal
1/2 teaspoon salt
1/4 teaspoon baking soda
1 egg, beaten
3/4 cup buttermilk
1 tablespoon shortening, melted

Brown the hamburger in a large skillet. Drain off the fat. Add the onion, Worcestershire sauce, chili powder, salt and tomato juice. Simmer for 5 minutes. Add the kidney beans. Place in a 1 1/2-quart casserole dish. Sift the cornmeal, salt and baking soda in a mixing bowl. Combine the egg and buttermilk. Blend with the dry ingredients. Add the shortening. Spoon over the hamburger mixture. Bake at 425 degrees for 25 to 30 minutes.

Slow Cooker Turkey and Dressing

8-ounce package herb-seasoned stuffing mix
1 onion, chopped
2 celery ribs, chopped
1 cup dried cranberries
3/4 cup chicken broth
3 tablespoons butter or margarine, melted
3 pounds frozen boneless turkey breast, thawed
1/4 teaspoon salt
1/2 teaspoon pepper
1/4 teaspoon dried thyme
1 package turkey gravy mix

Coat the inside of a 4-quart electric slow cooker with cooking spray. Add the stuffing mix, onion, celery and cranberries. Combine the broth and butter in a small bowl. Pour over the stuffing and stir gently. Remove the string from the turkey breast. Rinse the turkey breast. Place the turkey in a slow cooker on top of the stuffing. Combine the salt, pepper and thyme; sprinkle over the turkey. Cover and cook on high for 1 hour. Reduce to low and cook 5 to 6 hours. Remove the turkey to a serving platter and spoon the stuffing around the turkey. Prepare the gravy according to the directions on the package and serve with the turkey.

Makes 5 to 6 servings.

A great alternative to roasting and basting a turkey during the busy holiday. This is my children's favorite dressing.

Hot Turkey Salad

4 cups chopped turkey
1 cup chopped celery
1 cup mayonnaise
10 3/4-ounce can cream of chicken or mushroom soup
1/4 cup chopped onion
1 cup sour cream
1/2 cup herb-seasoned stuffing mix

Combine all the ingredients except the stuffing mix. Mix well. Pour into a glass baking dish. Top with the dressing. Bake at 375 degrees for 25 minutes.

Chicken Breast and Rice

1 stick margarine, melted
1 1/2 cups rice
4-ounce can sliced mushrooms, drained
10 3/4-ounce can French onion soup
8-ounce can water chestnuts, sliced
4 chicken breasts

Combine the margarine, rice, mushrooms, soup and water chestnuts. Pour into a casserole dish. Place the chicken breasts on top of the rice mixture. Cover with foil. Bake at 350 degrees for 45 minutes. Uncover and cook 10 minutes more.

Rita drinking tea

Cream Cheese and Spinach-Stuffed Chicken Rolls

6 boneless chicken breasts, cut in half
8-ounce package cream cheese, softened
1/2 cup chopped, cooked spinach, drained
1 small clove garlic, minced
1/8 teaspoon nutmeg
Salt and pepper to taste
1 large egg, beaten with 1 tablespoon water
1/2 cup unseasoned bread crumbs
3 tablespoons butter, melted

Flatten the chicken between sheets of plastic wrap to uniform 1/4-inch thickness. Beat the cream cheese with spinach, garlic, nutmeg, salt and pepper in a large bowl until combined. Spoon equal amounts of the mixture across the narrow end of each breast. Roll jelly roll style; secure with toothpicks. Dip in the egg, then roll in the bread crumbs, shaking off the excess. Arrange the chicken in one layer in a baking dish, seam side down. Drizzle with the butter. Bake at 375 degrees for 25 to 30 minutes or until golden.

Makes 6 servings.

Several years ago we organized a ladies stock club. We named it the PMS (Profit Makers Stock club). The first few years we studied and learned about buying and selling stock. Lately, we meet for potluck lunch. One of the members, Ann Bendell, brought this dish and shared the recipe.

Bombay Chicken

8 chicken breast halves
Salt
Paprika
All-purpose flour
4 tablespoons oil
1 cup sherry
4 tablespoons brown sugar
2 tablespoons soy sauce
4 tablespoons oil
1 teaspoon ginger
4 teaspoons sesame seeds
Peaches for garnish

Rinse and dry the chicken pieces. Season with the salt, paprika and sprinkle with flour. Brown on both sides in the hot oil. Remove the pieces to a 9x13-inch baking pan. Combine the sherry, brown sugar, soy sauce, oil, ginger and sesame seeds in a medium bowl. Mix well. Pour over the chicken. Cover the pan with foil. Bake at 375 degrees for 45 minutes or until tender. To serve, arrange the chicken on a platter and garnish with peach halves on top.

Makes 8 servings.

Vegetarian Bean Patties

15 1/2-ounce can white beans, drained and rinsed
1 tablespoon lemon juice
1 egg, beaten
1/3 cup bread crumbs
2 tablespoons grated Parmesan cheese
1 plum tomato
2 tablespoons chopped celery
2 tablespoons chopped green pepper
2 tablespoons chopped onion
1/4 teaspoon garlic salt
1/4 teaspoon hot pepper sauce
2 tablespoons tartar sauce

Mash the beans in a mixing bowl. Add the lemon juice and egg. Beat well. Add the remaining ingredients except the tartar sauce. Mix well. Shape into patties. Coat the skillet with cooking spray. Cook 8 minutes. Top with the tartar sauce.

Shrimp and Grits, Charleston Style

4 cups chicken broth
2 cups stone-ground yellow grits
Salt and pepper to taste
2 tablespoons sour cream
6 ounces chopped bacon
1 small onion, chopped
2 cups diced tomatoes
1 cup chopped scallions
1 teaspoon minced garlic
Pinch of basil
1/2 quart heavy cream
25 cooked shrimp

Bring the broth to a boil in a large saucepan. Add the grits, salt and pepper. Stir. Boil until smooth. Add the sour cream. Reduce the heat. Cook the chopped bacon in a large stockpot over a medium heat until brown and crisp. Drain. Add the onions, tomato, scallions, garlic and basil. Cook about 5 minutes or until soft. Add the cream. Reduce the heat to low and stir until thick. Add the shrimp. Serve over the grits.

Makes 6 servings.

Pumpkin Chili

1 medium pumpkin, 4 or 5 pounds or
2 cups solid pack pumpkin
1 small yellow onion, chopped
1 clove garlic, minced
1 red bell pepper, cored and diced
2 tablespoons vegetable oil
1 pound lean ground turkey or beef
4 cups diced tomatoes
2 cups tomato sauce
2 cups cooked kidney beans
1 cup whole kernel corn
1/2 cup diced green chilies
1 tablespoon chili powder
1 teaspoon ground cumin
Salt and fresh black pepper

If you don't want your family to know how nutritious this is, serve it as regular chili in a bowl. You will smile knowing that the bright orange color of pumpkin is loaded with an important antioxidant, beta-carotene. Eating a diet rich in foods containing beta-carotene may reduce the risk of developing certain types of cancer and offers protection against heart disease. But the best thing about pumpkin—it offers protection against some degenerative aspects of aging!

Cut the lid off the top of the pumpkin and set aside. Remove the seeds and pith and replace the lid. Bake at 375 degrees for 20 minutes. Scoop out the pumpkin flesh, leaving at least 1/2 inch to hold the pumpkin shape. Dice the pumpkin and set aside. Reserve the pumpkin shell. Sauté the onion, garlic and bell pepper in oil in a 6-quart saucepan for 5 minutes or until tender. Add ground meat and cook, stirring, until browned. Drain. Add tomatoes, tomato sauce, reserved pumpkin (2 to 3 cups fresh or 2 cups canned), kidney beans, corn, chilies, chili powder, cumin, salt and pepper. Bring to a boil; reduce the heat, cover and simmer for 30 minutes or desired consistency. Stir often. Adjust the seasoning. Serve from the reserved pumpkin shell. Garnish if desired with shredded cheese and sour cream. Serve over cooked rice.

One Skillet Lasagna

1 pound ground beef
1 envelope spaghetti sauce mix
16-ounce container creamed cottage cheese
3 cups egg noodles, uncooked
2 teaspoons basil leaves
1 tablespoon parsley flakes
1 teaspoon salt
16-ounce can diced tomatoes
8-ounce can tomato sauce
1 cup water
8 ounces shredded mozzarella cheese

Brown the beef in large skillet and drain. Sprinkle with 1/2 of the spaghetti sauce mix. Spoon the cottage cheese over the meat. Top with the noodles and the remaining spaghetti sauce mix, basil, parsley and salt. Pour the tomatoes, tomato sauce and water over the top making sure all ingredients are moistened. Bring to a boil, cover, lower the temperature and simmer for 35 minutes. Sprinkle with the cheese, and let stand for 5 minutes before serving.

The noodles don't have to be cooked separately!

Baked Spaghetti

1 pound ground beef
1 small onion, chopped
Three 8-ounce cans tomato sauce
1 cup water
1/4 teaspoon oregano
1/4 teaspoon basil
1/4 teaspoon rosemary
1/4 teaspoon marjoram
Dash of garlic salt
1 tablespoon sugar
1/4 teaspoon salt
1/4 teaspoon pepper
1/2 pound spaghetti, broken in 2-inch lengths, cooked and drained
1/4 pound grated or shredded Cheddar cheese

Brown the ground beef and onion in a skillet and drain. Add the tomato sauce, water, oregano, basil, rosemary, marjoram, garlic salt, sugar, salt and pepper. Simmer, covered, for 35 to 40 minutes. Place the spaghetti in the bottom of a 9x13-inch coated baking dish. Add 1/2 of the cheese to the sauce and pour over the spaghetti. Bake, covered, at 350 degrees for 45 minutes. Uncover and sprinkle the remaining cheese over the top and bake an additional 30 minutes. Serve with green tossed salad and French bread.

Serves 6 to 8.

Three Cheese Chicken Casserole

5-ounce package noodles
1/2 cup chopped green pepper
1/2 cup chopped onion
3 tablespoons butter
10 3/4-ounce can cream of mushroom soup
1/2 cup milk
6-ounce can sliced mushrooms, drained
1 1/2 cups chopped, cooked chicken breast
12-ounce carton creamed cottage cheese
10-ounce package grated Cheddar cheese
1/2 cup shredded Parmesan cheese
Paprika for garnish

Cook the noodles according to package directions and drain. Sauté the green pepper and onion in butter in a skillet. Remove from the heat. Stir in the soup, milk and mushrooms. Combine the soup mixture, noodles, chicken, cottage cheese and Cheddar cheese in a large bowl. Pour the mixture into a coated 9x13-inch casserole dish. Sprinkle the Parmesan cheese over the top and garnish with a small amount of the paprika. Bake at 350 degrees for 45 minutes.

This dish freezes well, so keep one in the freezer in case you have unexpected guests drop in or need an emergency dish for friends or family.

vegetables & sides

Herb Carrots

1 1/2 pounds carrots (8 large carrots) or two 15-ounce cans carrots, drained
1/4 cup water
1/2 teaspoon salt
1/2 cup butter, melted
1 teaspoon basil
1/2 teaspoon thyme
1 teaspoon lemon juice
1 small clove garlic, minced

Peel and wash the carrots. Slice in equal rounds. Combine the water and salt in a 1 1/2-quart glass dish. Add the carrots. Cover. Microwave on high for 7 to 8 minutes, stirring halfway through. Let sit 5 minutes, covered. Mix the butter, basil, thyme, lemon juice and garlic in a small bowl. Pour over the carrots and microwave 1 minute.

Makes 4 to 6 servings.

Exciting things happen to vegetables that are cooked in the microwave. These carrots are picture perfect. Add the herbs and they become gourmet!

Broccoli Casserole

Two 10-ounce packages frozen chopped broccoli, cooked and drained
10 3/4-ounce can cream of mushroom soup
1/2 cup mayonnaise
1 tablespoon lemon juice
1/2 cup grated cheese
1 ounce pimentos
1 cup crushed cheese crackers

Arrange the broccoli in a buttered 1 1/2-quart casserole dish. Combine the soup, mayonnaise, lemon juice and cheese in a medium size bowl. Spread over the broccoli. Top with the pimentos and crackers. Bake at 350 degrees for 20 minutes or until bubbly.

Makes 6 to 8 servings.

My friend Ruby Purkey brought this to many potluck dinners. She always went home with an empty dish, so I knew it was good. It's quick and easy to make.

Green Bean Casserole

Two 16-ounce cans French-style green beans, drained
Two 10 3/4-ounce cans cream of mushroom soup
2 1/2-ounce jar mushroom slices
1/2 cup slivered almonds, toasted
1 teaspoon Worcestershire sauce
1/8 teaspoon onion salt
1 cup grated sharp Cheddar cheese
3-ounce can French-fried onions

Combine the green beans, soup, mushrooms, almonds, Worcestershire sauce and onion salt in a medium bowl; mix well. Place the mixture in a 1 1/2-quart casserole dish and top with the cheese. Bake at 350 degrees for 30 to 35 minutes or until bubbly. Remove from the oven and top with the French-fried onions.

Spring Peas and Green Onions

1 tablespoon unsalted butter
1 large bunch green onions, coarsely chopped, including some of the top
3 cups fresh or frozen green peas
1/2 teaspoon salt
1/2 cup water

Melt the butter in a medium saucepan and add the green onions. Sauté for about 5 minutes or until wilted, being careful not to let them brown. Add the peas and sprinkle with the salt. Add the water, cover and simmer for about 10 minutes or until the peas are tender. Timing will depend on age and size of the peas and if they are fresh or frozen. Frozen peas take only a few minutes. When the peas are almost tender, if there is too much liquid, uncover, turn the heat to high and quickly boil some of the liquid down. Serve immediately.

If you are not a green-onion fancier, omit them and simply serve the peas buttered.

Vegetable Trio and Zippy Sauce

14 1/2-ounce can French-style green beans
15-ounce can small peas
15-ounce can baby lima beans
1 cup mayonnaise
3 tablespoons prepared mustard
2 tablespoons lemon juice
2 tablespoons minced onions
2 to 3 shakes Worcestershire sauce

Drain half of the liquid from each can of vegetables. Pour the vegetables into a saucepan. Cook over a medium heat until tender. Drain the remaining liquid. Combine the mayonnaise, mustard, lemon juice, onions and Worcestershire sauce in another saucepan. Heat until bubbly. Pour over the vegetables to serve.

Makes 8 to 10 servings.

Beets with Pineapple

2 tablespoons brown sugar
1 tablespoon cornstarch
1/2 teaspoon salt
14-ounce can pineapple chunks, drained, reserving juice
1 tablespoon lemon juice
1 tablespoon margarine
15-ounce can sliced beets, drained

Combine the brown sugar, cornstarch and salt in a large saucepan. Stir in the pineapple juice. Cook until the mixture thickens and bubbles, stirring constantly. Add the pineapple chunks, lemon juice, margarine, and beets. Cook over a medium heat until thoroughly heated.

Makes 6 servings.

Baked Pineapple

Two 15 1/4-ounce cans pineapple chunks, drained
3/4 cup sugar
1 tablespoon flour
1 egg, beaten
1 package butter flavored crackers, crushed
1 stick margarine, melted

Combine the pineapple, sugar, flour and egg. Pour into a 8 x 8-inch buttered baking dish. Combine the crackers and butter and sprinkle over the pineapple mixture. Bake at 325 degrees for approximately 1 hour.

Baked Honey Tomatoes

8 ripe medium tomatoes
1/2 cup coarse bread crumbs
2 teaspoons salt
2 teaspoons freshly ground black pepper
1 tablespoon dried tarragon
4 teaspoons honey
4 teaspoons unsalted butter

Slice off the stem ends of the tomatoes and carefully scoop out the seeds. Place the tomatoes open side up in a buttered baking dish. Combine the bread crumbs, salt, pepper and tarragon. Drizzle the honey over the tomatoes, rubbing it into the cavities. Sprinkle the tomatoes with the crumb mixture and dot with the butter. Bake, uncovered, at 350 degrees for 30 minutes or until the tomato skins begin to wrinkle. Place under the broiler for an additional 5 minutes or until the crumbs begin to brown. Serve hot or at room temperature.

Tomatoes and honey are always plentiful in Kentucky. You may not realize how well the flavors of tomato and honey go together. These are easy and once cooked may even wait if the family or guests are a little late for the meal.

Tomato-Pesto Tart

1 refrigerated piecrusts
2 cups shredded mozzarella cheese, divided
5 plum tomatoes, sliced
1/2 cup mayonnaise
1/4 cup grated Parmesan cheese
2 tablespoons basil pesto
1/2 teaspoon freshly ground pepper
3 tablespoons chopped fresh basil

Unfold the piecrust on a lightly coated baking sheet and roll into a 12-inch circle. Brush outer 1 inch of the crust with water. Fold the edges up and crimp and prick the bottom. Bake at 425 degrees for 8 to 10 minutes . Remove from the oven and sprinkle with 1 cup of the mozzarella cheese; let cool 15 minutes. Arrange the tomato slices over the cheese.

Combine the mayonnaise, Parmesan cheese, basil pesto, pepper, and the remaining mozzarella cheese in a large bowl. Spread evenly over the tomato slices. Bake at 375 degrees for 20 to 25 minutes. Remove from oven; sprinkle with basil.

You can make your own fresh basil pesto by processing 1 cup fresh basil, 1/2 cup chopped walnuts or pine nuts, 1 tablespoon olive oil, 1 garlic clove and 1/4 teaspoon salt in the food processor or blender until blended. There are also some nice jars of prepared pesto or dried packages available in the supermarket.

The bride at our first wedding reception brought me this recipe and asked me to serve it. It has been a hit ever since.

Charmed Potatoes

6 medium potatoes, peeled and sliced
2 tablespoons oil
2 tablespoons all-purpose flour
1/2 teaspoon salt
1 cup milk
1/2 cup processed cheese
10 3/4-ounce can cream of mushroom soup
2-ounce jar pimentos
1 medium onion, chopped
1/2 green pepper, diced
Salt and pepper to taste

Place the potatoes in a 1 1/2-quart saucepan. Parboil in salt water until tender. Combine the oil, flour, salt and milk in a glass mixing bowl. Microwave on high for 2 to 4 minutes or until the mixture starts to thicken, stirring after each minute. Add the cheese and microwave 1 minute. Add the soup, pimentos, onion, green pepper, salt and pepper to the cheese sauce. Mix thoroughly. Drain the potatoes and place in a buttered casserole dish. Pour the cheese sauce over the potatoes. Bake at 350 degrees for 25 to 30 minutes.

Makes 8 to 10 servings.

This is my favorite potato dish for Christmas. The red pimentos and green pepper make it very festive. I made this recipe at the Eastern Kentucky University home management house in 1970 and have used it every Christmas since.

Gourmet Potatoes

6 medium potatoes
3 cups shredded Cheddar cheese
1/4 cup plus 2 tablespoons butter
1 1/2 cups sour cream
1/3 cup chopped green onions
1 teaspoon salt
1/4 teaspoon pepper
Paprika

Cover the unpeeled potatoes with water in a large pan. Cook until the potatoes are soft. Peel and shred when cooled. Combine the cheese and 1/4 cup butter in a saucepan over a low heat. Stir occasionally until almost melted. Remove from the heat and blend in the sour cream, onions, salt and pepper. Fold in the potatoes. Place in a 2-quart casserole dish. Top with 2 tablespoons butter. Sprinkle with the paprika. Bake uncovered at 350 degrees for 40 minutes.

Makes 8 servings.

Potato Casserole

1/2 stick margarine, melted
1 small onion, chopped
1/2 cup chopped celery
8 ounces sour cream
1 cup grated Cheddar cheese
1 pound hash brown potatoes
10 3/4-ounce can cream of chicken soup
1/2 cup butter
Bacon bits, optional

Combine all the ingredients, except the bacon bits, in a large mixing bowl. Pour into a buttered 9x13-inch casserole dish. Dot with the butter. Bake at 350 degrees for 1 hour. Sprinkle the bacon bits on top.

This is a great potluck dish for a crowd.

Orange-Glazed Sweet Potatoes

29-ounce can sweet potatoes or yams
1/2 cup brown sugar, firmly packed
1 tablespoon cornstarch
1 cup orange juice
1 cup raisins
1/4 cup butter or margarine, melted
3 tablespoons chopped walnuts

Arrange the sweet potatoes in a lightly coated 9x13-inch baking dish. Combine the brown sugar and cornstarch in a bowl. Stir in the orange juice and raisins. Bring to a boil in the microwave, about 6 minutes. Cook, stirring occasionally, until the mixture thickens. Stir in the butter. Pour over the sweet potatoes. Sprinkle the walnuts on top. Bake uncovered at 350 degrees for 20 minutes.

Makes 4 to 6 servings.

Sweet Potato Delight

3 cups mashed sweet potatoes
1 cup sugar
1 cup coconut
2 eggs, beaten
1/2 cup butter, softened
1/2 cup milk
1 teaspoon vanilla extract
1 cup brown sugar
1/2 cup all-purpose flour
1 cup chopped pecans
1/2 cup butter, softened

Combine the mashed potatoes, sugar, coconut, eggs, 1/2 cup butter, milk and vanilla in a large mixing bowl. Mix well. Pour into a 2-quart baking dish. Combine the brown sugar, flour, pecans and remaining butter in another bowl. Crumble over the sweet potato mixture. Bake at 350 degrees for 30 minutes.

Corn Pudding

2 cups corn, fresh, canned or frozen
4 tablespoons all-purpose flour
2 teaspoons sugar
1 teaspoon salt
2 eggs, well beaten
1 tablespoon butter or margarine, melted
2 cups milk

Combine the corn, flour, sugar and salt in a mixing bowl. Combine the eggs, butter and milk in another bowl. Add to the corn mixture. Pour into a coated 2-quart baking dish. Bake at 350 degrees for 1 hour. Stir from the bottom 2 or 3 times during the first 30 minutes of baking time.

We can always count on my sister, Judy, to bring her corn pudding to family gatherings. It's Good!

Orange Zested Grits

3 cups water
1 teaspoon salt
1 cup quick-cooking grits, uncooked
1/4 cup butter or margarine
1 teaspoon grated orange rind
1 cup orange juice
4 eggs, beaten
2 tablespoons brown sugar

Bring the water and salt to a boil in a saucepan. Add the grits. Cook over a medium heat for 3 to 5 minutes, stirring constantly. Remove from the heat. Add the butter, orange rind, orange juice and eggs. Mix well. Pour into coated 1 1/2-quart baking dish. Sprinkle with the brown sugar. Bake at 350 degrees for 45 minutes or until a knife inserted in the center comes out clean.

Baked Garlic Cheese Grits

4 cups water
1 teaspoon salt
1 cup quick-cooking grits, uncooked
1/2 cup butter or margarine
6-ounce roll garlic cheese
2 eggs, beaten
1/2 cup milk

Bring the water and salt to a boil in a saucepan. Add the grits. Cook over a medium heat for 3 to 5 minutes, stirring constantly. Add the butter and cheese when thickened. Mix thoroughly until melted. Stir in the eggs and milk. Pour into coated 11x7-inch baking dish. Bake at 350 degrees for 45 minutes.

This can be refrigerated before baking.

Serves 8.

Curried Rice

1 1/3 cups uncooked rice
1/2 tablespoon curry powder
3 tablespoons finely chopped onion
2 tablespoons butter or margarine
1 teaspoon salt
1 tablespoon wine vinegar
1/3 cup slivered almonds, toasted
1 cup finely chopped celery
1/3 cup chopped raisins
1 cup green peas, cooked
1/4 cup mayonnaise

Prepare the rice according to the package directions. Cook the curry powder, onions and butter in a saucepan until the onions are soft but not brown. Add to the hot rice. Add the salt, vinegar, almonds, celery and raisins. Mix well. Chill 3 hours. Stir in the peas and mayonnaise. Pack in individual molds. Turn out on a lettuce leaf placed on individual plates to serve. Serve with Bombay Chicken on page 98.

Makes 8 servings.

Apple Casserole

6 to 8 apples, peeled and sliced
1 tablespoon lemon juice
2 tablespoons water
3/4 cup sugar
1/2 cup all-purpose flour
1 1/2 teaspoons cinnamon
1/4 teaspoon salt
1/4 cup butter, cut in pats
1 cup grated sharp Cheddar cheese

Place the apples, lemon juice and water in a 1 1/2-quart glass baking dish. Combine the sugar, flour, cinnamon and salt in a another bowl. Sprinkle over the apples. Place the butter on the topping mixture. Sprinkle with the grated cheese. Bake, uncovered, at 350 degrees for 30 minutes.

Makes 6 to 8 servings.

This is a great side dish for pork. It creates some good conversation as folks are a little unsure about the combination of cheese, apples and cinnamon, but they love the taste.

Tomato Grits

2 cups water
1 1/4 cups milk
1 cup quick-cooking grits, uncooked
Salt to taste
1 medium onion, chopped
3 cloves garlic, minced
4 ounces Mexican-style processed cheese spread
14-ounce can tomatoes with green chiles

Bring the water and milk to a boil in a saucepan. Add the grits and salt, stirring constantly. Reduce the heat, cover and cook 3 to 5 minutes. Sauté the onion and garlic in a small skillet until clear. Stir into the grits. Add the cheese and stir until melted. Add the tomatoes. Pour the mixture into a buttered 2-quart casserole dish. Bake at 350 degrees for 40 minutes.

Serves 8.

This is a great side dish for pork. It's a little on the spicy side, but oh, so tasty!

desserts & sweets

202

Pineapple Cream Pie

1 baked pie shell — 1/4 teaspoon salt
3 egg yolks — 1 cup milk
2/3 cup sugar — 1 cup crushed pineapple
1/3 cup flour — 1 tablespoon butter
2 tablespoons lemon juice

Beat yolks, add sugar, flour and salt. Add milk and pineapple. [illegible] boiler until thick and creamy. Stir frequently. Add butter and juice. Pour into pie shell.

Meringue

3 eggs (whites) — 5 tablespoons sugar

Beat whites until stiff. Add sugar and beat until creamy. Roughly spread on filling. Bake 12 minutes in moderately slow oven.

Recipes are found in many forms, on the back of envelopes, napkins, newspaper clippings, stuffed in drawers, books and boxes. James Neale, a 90-year old Richmond Main Street resident who grew up across the street from the Bennett House, shared his favorite Pineapple Cream Pie recipe. He penned this copy in his mother's cookbook when he was 16 years old. It has become a Bennett House signature dessert, thanks to Mr. Neale.

Chocolate Chip Cake

18 1/4-ounce box yellow cake mix
3.4-ounce box instant vanilla pudding
3.9-ounce box instant chocolate pudding
4 eggs
1 1/2 cups water
1/2 cup oil
6-ounce package semisweet chocolate chips
Powdered sugar

Combine the cake mix, vanilla pudding and chocolate pudding in a large mixing bowl. Add the eggs, water and oil. Blend well. Beat for 2 minutes at medium speed. Fold in the chocolate chips. Bake in a coated and floured bundt pan at 350 degrees for 65 minutes. Cool 20 minutes and remove from the pan. Sprinkle with the powdered sugar.

Sunflower Pound Cake

18 1/4-ounce box lemon cake mix
3.4-ounce box instant vanilla pudding
4 eggs
1 cup water
1/3 cup oil

Mix all the ingredients for 2 minutes on medium speed. Pour into a coated bundt pan. Bake at 350 degrees for 50 to 60 minutes.

Orange Juice Cake

18 1/4-ounce box yellow butter cake mix
3.4-ounce box vanilla instant pudding mix
1 1/4 cup orange juice, divided
1/2 cup oil
4 eggs
1/2 cup sugar
1/2 cup margarine

Combine the cake mix, pudding mix, 1 cup of the orange juice, oil and eggs. Mix on medium speed for 2 minutes. Pour into a coated and floured bundt pan. Bake at 350 degrees for 40 to 50 minutes. Combine the remaining orange juice, sugar and margarine in a small bowl and place in a microwave on high for 2 minutes. Stir. Pour over the hot cake in the pan. Let set until cool.

This Orange Juice Cake was a favorite of Franklin County Extension Homemakers and always gets rave reviews because it is so moist.

Apple Cake with Butter Sauce

1 cup unsalted butter
2 cups granulated sugar
2 eggs
2 cups thick applesauce
1 teaspoon vanilla extract
3 cups flour
1 teaspoon cinnamon
1 teaspoon freshly grated nutmeg
2 teaspoons baking soda

Cream the butter and sugar in a mixing bowl until fluffy. Beat in one egg at a time. Stir in the applesauce and vanilla. Sift the flour, cinnamon, nutmeg and soda in medium bowl. Add the flour mixture, gradually, to the applesauce and blend thoroughly. Pour evenly into a coated and floured 10-inch tube pan. Bake at 325 degrees for 1 hour 10 minutes. Cool in the pan for 15 minutes. Serve with Hot Butter Sauce over the cake.

Hot Butter Sauce

1/2 cup unsalted butter
1 cup sugar
1/2 cup heavy whipping cream
1 teaspoon bourbon

Melt the butter in a small saucepan. Add the sugar, cream and bourbon. Bring to a boil slowly. Stir until the sugar is dissolved. Remove from the heat. Cool slightly and serve over Apple Cake.

Hickory Nut Cake

3/4 cup butter
2 cups sugar
4 eggs, separated and beaten
2 teaspoons baking powder
3 cups flour, sifted
1/2 cup milk
1 teaspoon vanilla extract
2 cups chopped hickory nuts

Cream the butter and sugar in a medium bowl. Add the egg yolks and baking powder to the flour in a separate bowl. Add the flour mixture and milk, alternately, to butter mixture. Pour in the vanilla extract. Fold in the egg whites and nuts. Pour into a 9x13-inch pan or bundt pan. Bake at 350 degrees for 1 hour.

Ice the cake with caramel icing. Sprinkle the top with whole or chopped nuts.

One of the best parts of fall is hickory nut hunting. I remember going out on the farm with my brother and sister every year to look for these delicacies. Picking the nuts out of the shell was the hard part. But it was certainly worth the effort as hickory nuts have the most wonderful flavor. If you are fortunate to have hickory nuts, guard them with your life! If not, substitute pecans for another wonderful treat.

Five-Flavored Pound Cake

1 cup butter
1/2 cup vegetable shortening
3 cups sugar
5 eggs, well beaten
3 cups all-purpose flour
1/2 teaspoon baking powder
1/4 teaspoon salt
1 cup milk
1 teaspoon coconut extract
1 teaspoon rum extract
1 teaspoon lemon extract
1 teaspoon vanilla extract
1 teaspoon butter extract

Cream the butter, shortening and sugar in a mixing bowl until light and fluffy. Mix in the eggs. Sift the flour, baking powder and salt together. Add the flour and milk, alternately, to the creamed mixture. Stir in the flavorings. Spoon into a coated and floured 10-inch tube pan. Bake at 325 degrees for 1 hour 30 minutes. Top with Pound Cake Glaze.

Makes 12 to 15 servings.

Pound Cake Glaze

1 cup sugar
1/2 cup water
1/2 teaspoon coconut extract
1/2 teaspoon rum extract
1/2 teaspoon lemon extract
1/2 teaspoon vanilla extract
1/2 teaspoon butter extract
1/2 teaspoon almond extract

Bring all the ingredients to a boil. Stir until the sugar is melted. Pour over the pound cake when taken out of oven. Let sit in the pan until the cake is cool.

This is a favorite recipe of the Richmond Altrusa Club. One of our club members, Jackie Goucher, shared the recipe.

Kentucky Bourbon Cake

18 1/4-ounce package yellow cake mix
3.4-ounce package instant vanilla pudding mix
4 eggs
1/2 cup oil
1/2 cup water
1/2 cup bourbon
1 cup chopped nuts
1/2 cup bourbon
1/2 cup butter
1/2 cup sugar

Combine the cake mix, pudding mix, eggs, oil, water and 1/2 cup bourbon for 1 minute on medium speed. Fold in the nuts. Pour into a coated tube pan and bake at 325 degrees for 50 to 55 minutes. Heat the 1/2 cup bourbon, butter and sugar in a heavy saucepan until the sugar is dissolved. Pour over the cake while still warm.

You may make a rum cake by using rum instead of bourbon.

Makes 12 to 16 servings.

Dump Cake

21-ounce can cherry pie filling
20-ounce can crushed pineapple, undrained
18 1/4-ounce box yellow cake mix
1 stick butter, softened and cut in pieces
1 cup coconut
Chopped pecans

Spread the pie filling in the bottom of a coated 9x13-inch pan. Spoon the pineapple over the pie filling. Sprinkle the cake mix on top of the pineapple. Place the butter on top of the cake mix. Top with the coconut and pecans. Bake at 350 degrees for 1 hour.

Actually dump everything on top of each ingredient - thus, the name "Dump Cake."

Old Fashioned Jam Cake

1 cup sugar
1 1/2 teaspoons cloves
1 1/2 teaspoons cinnamon
1 1/2 teaspoons allspice
1 cup oil
3 eggs, well beaten
1 1/2 cups jam
1 1/2 teaspoons baking soda
1 cup buttermilk
2 cups flour
1 cup chopped nuts

Combine the sugar, spices and oil in a large mixing bowl. Add the eggs and jam. Mix well. Stir the soda into the buttermilk. Add the flour and buttermilk, alternately, to the batter. Fold in the nuts. Coat and flour a 10-inch tube pan or line with parchment paper. Bake at 350 degrees for 55 minutes. Remove from the pan after 10 minutes. Cool before frosting with Easy Caramel Icing.

Easy Caramel Icing

1/2 cup butter
1 cup brown sugar, firmly packed
1/4 cup milk
1 3/4 to 2 cups powdered sugar, sifted

Melt the butter in a saucepan. Add the brown sugar. Bring to a boil. Boil over a low heat for two minutes, stirring constantly. Stir in the milk. Bring to a boil, stirring constantly. Cool to lukewarm. Add the powdered sugar gradually. Beat until thick enough to spread. If too stiff, add a small amount of water.

Strawberry Cake

18 1/4-ounce box white cake mix
3-ounce package strawberry gelatin
3/4 cup oil
1/2 cup water
4 eggs
12 ounces frozen strawberries, thawed and 1/3 cup reserved

Blend the cake mix, gelatin, oil and water in a large bowl with a mixer. Add the eggs one at a time. Stir in the strawberries. Pour into a coated and floured 9x13-inch baking dish. Bake at 350 degrees for 35 minutes. Glaze while warm.

Strawberry Cake Glaze

1 stick butter
1-pound box powdered sugar
1/3 cup reserved strawberries

Melt the butter in a saucepan. Add the sugar and strawberries. Pour over the warm cake.

This was my daughter Angela's favorite cake. She would always ask for it for her birthday.

Lemon Jewels

18 1/4-ounce box lemon supreme cake mix
1 egg
2 tablespoons lemon juice
8-ounce container whipped topping, thawed
Powdered sugar

Mix the ingredients in a large bowl. Drop by teaspoonfuls onto a plate covered with powdered sugar. Roll into balls. Place the balls on a coated baking sheet and bake at 350 degrees for 8 to 10 minutes. Cookies won't be brown on top; check doneness by gently lifting to see if the bottom is brown. Do not overbake. Cookies will be soft. Cool 10 minutes on baking sheet.

Makes 65 to 75 cookies.

Butter Pecan Brownies

18 1/4-ounce box butter pecan cake mix
2 sticks margarine, softened
2 eggs
8-ounce package cream cheese, softened
1/2-pound box powdered sugar
Chopped pecans

Combine the cake mix, 1 stick margarine and 1 egg with a fork in a mixing bowl. Place in a coated 9x13-inch baking pan lined with foil. Mix the cream cheese, 1 stick margarine, 1 egg and powdered sugar in another bowl. Pour over the cake mixture. Sprinkle with the pecans. Bake at 350 degrees for 35 minutes. Cool completely. Lift the foil out of the pan for easy cutting and cut into bite-size pieces.

Makes 60.

Setting up beautiful details in your home can make an enormous difference to the quality of your life. Each room in the Bennett House offers a special collection of beautiful details which one guest described as "eye gifts" to view and enjoy during their stay. If you have pretty linens, dishes or family keepsakes hidden away, bring them out for your own special gallery show. Take time to look at the simplest detail, think about the family before you that used these precious items, then share them with your friends and family before it's too late!

Blueberry Peach Trifle

14-ounce can sweetened condensed milk
1 1/2 cups cold water
2 teaspoons grated lemon rind
3.4-ounce package instant vanilla pudding
2 cups whipped cream
4 cups pound cake cubes
1 pound fresh peaches, peeled and chopped
2 cups fresh blueberries or strawberries, rinsed

Combine the sweetened condensed milk, water and lemon rind in a large bowl. Mix well. Add the pudding mix. Beat until well blended. Chill 5 minutes. Fold in the whipped cream. Spoon 2 cups of the pudding mixture into a 4-quart glass serving bowl. Layer in the following order: half of the cake cubes, peaches, half of the remaining pudding mixture, the remaining cake cubes and blueberries. Top with the remaining pudding mixture, spreading to 1 inch of the edge of the bowl. Chill 4 hours. Garnish with blueberries and strawberries.

Pumpkin Dip

8-ounce package cream cheese, softened
2 cups powdered sugar
15-ounce can pumpkin
1 teaspoon ground ginger
1 teaspoon allspice
2 teaspoons cinnamon

Blend the cream cheese and sugar in a medium bowl. Stir in the pumpkin, ginger, allspice and cinnamon.

Makes about 3 cups.

I serve this in a cream crystal pumpkin shaped bowl with ginger snaps or graham cracker bits. It's always a hit.

Chocolate Mousse Tarts

24 vanilla wafers or ginger snaps
8-ounce package cream cheese, softened
3-ounce package cream cheese, softened
2/3 cup sugar
6 large eggs
Eight 1-ounce squares semisweet chocolate, melted
1/3 cup whipping cream
1 tablespoon vanilla extract
Sweetened whipped cream
Chocolate syrup
Maraschino cherries

Line muffin pans with 24 paper liners. Place a vanilla wafer in each liner; set aside. Beat the cream cheese in a large mixing bowl at medium speed with an electric mixer until creamy. Add the sugar, gradually, beating well. Add the eggs, one at a time, beating after each addition. Add the melted chocolate, whipping cream and vanilla. Beat at a low speed until blended. Spoon evenly into the liners. Bake at 325 degrees for 14 to 16 minutes. Cool, cover and chill. Pipe or dollop the sweetened whipped cream onto the center of the tarts and drizzle with chocolate syrup to serve. Garnish with a cherry.

Peanut Butter Crunch Pie

1/3 cup corn syrup
1/3 cup peanut butter
2 cups crisp rice cereal
Ice cream, softened

Combine the corn syrup and peanut butter in a medium bowl. Mix thoroughly. Add the cereal and stir until well-coated. Line the sides and bottom of a 9-inch pie plate evenly with mixture. Press with an 8-inch pie plate. Chill until firm. Spread the ice cream evenly into the crust. Remove the pie slices easily by placing a wet towel under and around the pie plate. Allow to stand a few minutes before serving. Top with Caramel Peanut Butter Sauce to serve.

Caramel Peanut Butter Sauce

1 cup brown sugar
1/3 cup milk
1/4 cup light corn syrup
2 teaspoons margarine
1/4 cup peanut butter
Peanuts or crushed peanut brittle for garnish

Combine the brown sugar, milk, corn syrup and margarine in a saucepan. Cook and stir over a medium heat until the sugar dissolves and the margarine melts. Remove from the heat and add the peanut butter. Beat until smooth. Serve over Peanut Butter Crunch Pie and garnish. A great sauce for vanilla ice cream.

Caramel Nut Sticks

1 stick margarine
2 cups light brown sugar
2 eggs
1 3/4 cups flour
2 teaspoons baking powder
1/2 teaspoon vanilla extract
3/4 cup chopped nuts

Combine the margarine and sugar in a mixing bowl. Stir in the eggs, flour, baking powder and vanilla. Add the nuts. Spread in a coated 9x13-inch pan. Bake at 350 degrees for 35 to 40 minutes. Cool and cut.

Coconut Sweets

1 1/2 sticks margarine
14-ounce can sweetened condensed milk
4 1/2 cups powdered sugar
14-ounce bag coconut
12 ounces chocolate chips
Paraffin

Melt the margarine and milk in a small saucepan. Combine this with the powdered sugar and coconut in a mixing bowl. Press the ingredients into a 9x13-inch pan. Refrigerate overnight. Cut into 1-inch squares. Heat the chocolate chips and a few shavings of paraffin in a double boiler. Dip the squares in the chocolate and place on waxed paper to cool.

Pretty presentations transform a signature dish into a work of art. Each Bennett House breakfast starts with the first course in a crystal sherbet with fresh flowers and homemade bread. When guests sit down to a beautiful table of fine china, crisp linens and sterling silver, they are transformed into another place and time. There's only one problem, they don't want to leave!

Frozen Orange Balls

12-ounce box vanilla wafers
3 cups powdered sugar
6-ounce can frozen orange juice concentrate, thawed
1/2 cup butter or 1 stick margarine, melted
1/2 cup chopped pecans
1/2 cup coconut

Crush the vanilla wafers in a food processor. Add the powdered sugar, orange juice, butter and pecans and mix well. Shape the dough into small balls and roll in the coconut. Freeze and serve frozen.

Makes 3 dozen.

A nice party and tea item to make ahead and freeze.

Strawberry Chews

1 pound shredded coconut
1/4 pound almonds
1 tablespoon sugar
15-ounce can sweetened condensed milk
1/2 teaspoon vanilla extract
Three 3-ounce packages strawberry flavored gelatin
Few drops red food coloring
Green powdered sugar frosting

Grind the coconut and almonds in a blender until fine. Add the sugar, milk, vanilla extract, 1 1/2 packages of the gelatin and food coloring and mix well. Shape into berries and roll in the remaining gelatin. Add stems and leaves using the green frosting. Store in airtight container or in freezer until ready to use.

A great little treat when strawberries are not in season.

Date Ritz Crackers

1 1/2 cups chopped dates
1 1/2 cups chopped pecans
14-ounce can sweetened condensed milk
Ritz crackers

Combine the dates, pecans and milk in a mixing bowl. Chill 3 to 4 hours or longer. Spread onto the Ritz crackers. Cover baking sheet with parchment paper. Bake at 350 degrees for 10 to 12 minutes. Cool. Top with Date Ritz Cracker Frosting.

Makes 120 crackers.

Date Ritz Cracker Frosting

Two 3-ounce packages cream cheese, softened
2 1/2 cups powdered sugar
1 teaspoon coconut flavoring

Mix well. Frost the Date Ritz Crackers.

This is a great sweet and salty combination. I keep the mixture in the refrigerator during the holidays and make crackers as needed when guests drop in.

Date Marshmallow Roll

1 tablespoon orange juice
1 cup dates, cut in eighths
1/8 teaspoon salt
1/4 cup chopped nuts
1/2 cup miniature marshmallows
1 cup whipped topping
1 1/2 cups graham cracker crumbs
3 tablespoons melted butter

Pour the range juice over the dates in a bowl and add the salt. Fold the dates, nuts and marshmallows into 1/2 cup of the whipped topping. Fold in the graham cracker crumbs, reserving about 1 tablespoon. Sprinkle the reserved crumbs on a sheet of buttered heavy waxed paper. Turn the date mixture onto the waxed paper and shape into a 6-inch roll, 3 inches in diameter. Roll in the waxed paper. Chill for at least 12 hours. Cut into approximately 3/4-inch slices. Serve garnished with the remaining whipped topping.

Serves 6 to 8.

The Date Marshmallow Roll was a favorite recipe shared in home economic circles during the late '50s. I first tasted this when my mother received the recipe from an Extension Homemaker club meeting. I had not used it for a number of years and recently ran across it in a Tennessee Home Economics cookbook. It's true what they say, "nothing new under the sun."

Acini Di Pepe Salad

2/3 cup acini di pepe macaroni
1/4 cup sugar
1 tablespoon flour
2 eggs, beaten
1/4 teaspoon salt
20-ounce can crushed pineapple, drained, reserving the juice
11-ounce can mandarin oranges, drained, reserving the juice
4 ounce chopped walnuts
8-ounce container frozen whipped topping, thawed
2 cups miniature marshmallows

Cook the macaroni according to the package directions; drain and set aside. combine the sugar, flour, eggs, salt and fruit juices in a 1-quart glass measuring cup. Microwave on high for two minutes. Stir and microwave for 1 minute or until thick. Cool, add the macaroni, pineapple, oranges and walnuts. Fold in the whipped topping and marshmallows. Refrigerate until ready to serve. Garnish with maraschino cherries.

My friend Nancy Wray introduced me to acini di pepe macaroni. I had never noticed it at the supermarket. This recipe came from her Aunt Reba's church friend in Lakeland, Florida. It is so light and refreshing. Sometimes I even serve it in stemware as a dessert. All ages seem to like it and try to figure out the ingredients. They are surprised when you tell them it is macaroni!

Frozen Fruit Salad

3/4 cup sugar
1/4 cup light corn syrup
2 cups water
2 tablespoons frozen orange juice concentrate
2 tablespoons frozen lemonade concentrate
1/4 watermelon, cut in bite-size or melon-ball pieces
1/2 cantaloupe, cut in bite-size pieces
1/2 honeydew melon, cut in bite-size pieces
1/4 pound red and green grapes, left whole
2 cups frozen peaches
2 cups frozen blackberries
2 cups frozen raspberries

Heat the sugar, corn syrup and water in a large saucepan until the sugar is dissolved. Remove from the heat and add the orange and lemon juice concentrates. Set aside to cool. Combine the watermelon, cantaloupe, honeydew melon, grapes and peaches in a large bowl. Add the frozen blackberries and raspberries. Pour the syrup over the fruit. Remove the fruit and place in 1-quart resealable bags. Freeze until ready to use. Remove from the freezer about 45 minutes before serving time. The fruit should be slushy.

Bennett House guests are always sharing recipes. This came from Tim Malone who stays so often that I call him my adopted son. This recipe is great for summer picnics. Take it out of the freezer and when you get to the outing, it's ready to serve! A great recipe for a crowd, this is easily doubled and everything is assembled and stored in freezer bags until ready to use.

Holiday Buckeyes

3 pounds powdered sugar
2 pounds smooth peanut butter
1 pound margarine, softened
24 ounces chocolate chips
Paraffin

Mix the sugar, peanut butter and margarine, by hand, in a large mixing bowl until smooth. Form into balls. Melt the chocolate chips and a few shavings of paraffin in a double boiler. Dip the candy into the chocolate and place on waxed paper to cool. Store in an airtight container.

Makes 75 to 80 candies.

Bennett House Devonshire Cream

2 cups unsalted butter, softened
8-ounce package cream cheese, softened
12 ounces whipped topping
2 cups powdered sugar
1 teaspoon clear vanilla extract

Beat the butter and cream cheese with an electric mixer until fluffy. Add the whipped topping and fold in the powdered sugar and vanilla. Refrigerate. Serve cold with warm scones.

Nancy Wray, Bennett House Tea Master

Charlotte Russe

3-ounce package unflavored gelatin
1 pint milk
1 cup sugar
3 egg yolks
1 teaspoon vanilla extract
1 quart heavy cream
1/4 cup whisky, sherry or vanilla extract, if desired
Two 3-ounce packages ladyfingers, split crosswise
1 cup chopped pecans
1 cup candied fruit

Dissolve the gelatin in about 1/4 cup of cold milk. Heat the remaining milk in the top of a double boiler. Add the sugar and gelatin and stir until both are dissolved. Beat the egg yolks in a separate bowl, adding a small portion of the hot-milk mixture to it. Add the egg yolk mixture to the milk in the double boiler and cook, stirring until thickened like custard. Fold in the vanilla extract and set aside to cool.

Whip the cream and flavoring in a separate bowl. Fold the whipped cream mixture into the custard. Line a bowl with the lady fingers and pour the custard over the ladyfingers. Trim the top with the chopped pecans or candied fruit. The pecans and fruit can be added to the custard mixture. Use a pastry brush to brush a small amount of the whipped cream around the bowl to help the ladyfingers stay in place. For an extra touch soak the fruit and chopped nuts in whisky or sherry before they are sprinkled on top.

My Bennett House "updated" version of this recipe is to line antique teacups with ladyfingers, fill with your favorite ice cream, and top with whipped cream. Place a silver teaspoon on the saucer and you've got a signature dessert. A favorite dessert for many Richmond women's groups.

Grasshopper Creams

1 stick margarine, softened
1 cup sugar
4 eggs,beaten
16 ounces chocolate syrup
1 cup flour
3-ounce package cream cheese, softened
1/2 stick margarine, softened
4 cups powdered sugar
4 tablespoon milk
3 teaspoons peppermint extract
Green food coloring
6-ounce package chocolate chips
1 stick margarine

Cream the 1 stick margarine and sugar. Add the eggs, chocolate syrup and flour and mix well. Pour into a coated 9x13-inch pan. Bake at 350 degrees for 25 minutes. Cool. Beat the cream cheese, 1/2 stick margarine, powdered sugar, milk, peppermint extract and food coloring until smooth. Spread over the cool cake. Refrigerate for 45 minutes. Microwave the chocolate chips with the 1 stick margarine on high for 1 minute. Stir until the chips are melted and smooth. Spread over the cooled mint layer. Keep refrigerated until ready to use. Cut in small squares.

Dip your knife in warm water before cutting to keep the top chocolate layer from cracking. Look for food coloring concentrated paste in the cake decorating section. One or two drops from a tooth pick will provide a nicer color and no bitter taste.

Use the green color for St. Patrick day and pink for weddings or showers.

Madison Cream (Strawberry Clotted Cream)

8-ounce package cream cheese, softened
1/2 cup sour cream
2 tablespoons strawberry extract
1/2 teaspoon vanilla extract
12-ounce container whipped topping, thawed
3/4 cup powdered sugar

Combine the cream cheese, sour cream, strawberry extract and vanilla extract in a medium bowl. Beat using an electric mixer on medium speed until well combined. Fold in the whipped topping and powdered sugar. Cover and chill.

Serve on hot scones or as a filling for prepared tart shells. When I am in a hurry, I use the store-bought cookie dough for easy-to-do tartlet shells. The sugar cookie dough is great with the Madison Cream. Roll the cookie dough into 1-inch balls. Press into bottom and halfway up sides of miniature muffin pans. Bake at 350 degrees for 12 minutes and remove from oven.

You can substitute chocolate chip cookie dough for the sugar cookie dough and change the Madison Cream to Bennett House Devonshire Cream. Spoon or pipe the cream mixture into cookie cups. Garnish with fresh strawberries, pink or white sugar and mint, if desired.

These make nice little desserts for showers or special tea times. So easy but so delightful.

Hot Caramel Sauce

1 cup butter
2 cups sugar
2 teaspoons lemon juice
1 1/2 cups whipping cream

Melt the butter in a saucepan. Add the sugar and lemon juice. Cook for 6 to 8 minutes or until it turns a deep caramel color, stirring constantly. Add the cream gradually and cook for 1 to 2 minutes, stirring constantly. Remove from the heat. Serve over bread pudding or ice cream.

Bugles Snack

Two 12 1/4-ounce packages Bugles
4 cups chopped nuts
2 tablespoons orange juice
2 egg whites
1 1/3 cups sugar
2 tablespoons cinnamon
1 tablespoon allspice
1 tablespoon ginger

Combine the bugles and nuts in large mixing bowl. Beat the orange juice and egg whites in another bowl using an electric mixer. Add the sugar, cinnamon, allspice and ginger to the egg whites. Pour over the bugles and nuts. Mix well. Spread in a baking dish and bake at 275 degrees for 45 minutes.

Pay Day Bars

18 1/4-ounce box yellow cake mix
1/3 cup margarine
1 egg
3 cups miniature marshmallows
2/3 cup corn syrup
1/4 cup margarine
2 teaspoons vanilla extract
2 cups peanut butter chips
2 cups salted peanuts
2 cups crisp rice cereal

Combine the cake mix, 1/3 cup margarine and egg in a large mixing bowl. Press into an uncoated 9x13-inch baking dish. Bake at 350 degrees for 12 to 15 minutes. Remove from the oven and sprinkle with the marshmallows. Return to the oven for 1 minute. Heat the corn syrup, 1/4 cup margarine, vanilla and peanut butter chips in a saucepan until the chips are melted. Remove from the heat. Stir in the peanuts and cereal. Spread over the marshmallows and chill. Cut into 2-inch bars.

Makes 50 bars.

This is my daughter Angela's favorite dessert to make for tailgating or pot luck dinners.

Brown Sugar Pecan Cookies

1 cup butter, softened
1/2 cup white sugar
1/2 cup brown sugar
1 egg
1 teaspoon vanilla extract
2 cups flour
1/2 teaspoon baking soda
1/4 teaspoon salt
1/2 cup chopped pecans

Beat the butter in a mixing bowl at medium speed. Add the sugars, egg and vanilla. Combine the flour, baking soda and salt in another bowl. Add to the butter mixture. Stir in the pecans. Chill the dough for 30 minutes. Shape into 1-inch balls. Place on an uncoated cookie sheet. Bake at 350 degrees for 10 to 12 minutes. Cool on wire rack. Frost with Brown Sugar Pecan Cookie Frosting. Sprinkle with pecans.

Makes 5 dozen.

Brown Sugar Pecan Cookie Frosting

1 cup brown sugar
1/2 cup milk
1 tablespoon margarine
1 1/2 to 1 2/3 cups powdered sugar

Combine the brown sugar and milk in a saucepan. Cook over a medium heat, stirring constantly until the mixture comes to a boil. Boil 4 minutes. Remove from the heat. Stir in the margarine. Add the powdered sugar and beat at medium speed until smooth. Spread on the Brown Sugar Pecan Cookies.

Orange Slice Cookies

1/2 cup shortening
1/2 cup butter
1 cup light brown sugar
1 cup sugar
1 teaspoon vanilla extract
2 eggs, beaten
1 cups flour
1/2 teaspoon salt
1/2 teaspoon baking soda
1 tablespoon baking powder
1 cup flaked coconut
1 cups quick-cooking oats
1 cup diced candy orange slices
1 cup chopped pecans
Whole pecans for garnish

Cream the shortening and butter in a large mixing bowl. Add the sugars and vanilla extract and beat thoroughly. Stir in the eggs until the mixture is fluffy. Blend in the flour, salt, baking soda and baking powder. Add the coconut, oats, orange slices and chopped pecans. Drop by teaspoonfuls, 1 inch apart, on an uncoated baking sheet. Top each cookie with a whole pecan. Bake at 400 degrees for 8 to 10 minutes. Cool on a wire rack.

Makes approximately 5 dozen.

Over the years I have experimented with various ways to cook drop cookies for even coloring, uniform size and overall appearance. Lining the cookie sheet with parchment paper produces a quality product but I prefer a baking stone for the best results.

Drop Sugar Cookies

1 cup butter
1 cup sugar
1 cup powdered sugar
1 cup vegetable oil
1 egg
4 cups plus 4 tablespoons flour
1 teaspoon cream of tartar
1 teaspoon baking soda
1 teaspoon almond extract
1/2 teaspoon salt

Cream the butter in a large mixing bowl. Add the sugar and powdered sugar and mix well. Add the oil and mix well. Add the eggs and almond extract and mix until blended. Sift the flour, cream of tartar, baking soda and salt in a separate bowl. Add to the sugar mixture and mix well. Let chill overnight.Roll into walnut-size pieces. Place on an uncoated baking sheet. Flatten with a small glass that has been dipped into sugar. Bake at 350 degrees for 8 to 10 minutes. Remove to a wire rack to cool.

Makes 6 dozen.

Be sure to use genuine almond extract, not imitation. Increase the baking time to 10 to 12 minutes when using an air bake cookie sheet.

These make the best caring and sharing cookies to take to shut-ins and special little ones. This recipe is from the kitchen of Mary Margaret Ricketts, a blue ribbon county fair winner.

No-Bake Cookies

1/2 cup margarine
2 cups sugar
1/3 cup cocoa
1/2 cup milk
2 1/2 cups quick-cooking oats
1 teaspoon vanilla extract
1 cup chopped nuts or flaked coconut
1/2 cup smooth peanut butter

Place margarine in a glass mixing bowl and cook in the microwave on high for 1 minute. Add the sugar, cocoa and milk and mix well. Cook in the microwave on high for 6 to 7 minutes or until bubbly. Stir in the oats, vanilla extract, nuts and peanut butter. Drop by teaspoonfuls onto waxed paper. Cool completely. Store in an airtight container.

Makes 5 dozen.

What child or adult doesn't just love no-bake cookies? This was one of the first recipes I adapted for microwave cooking. I still make them that way.

Holiday Cookie Swap

What would the holidays be without an annual cookie swap? Each member of the Modern Homemakers Club would bring five or six dozen cookies of the same recipe and then go home with five dozen of different kinds. Some groups get together and bake the cookies but we always spent the time together tasting everyone's favorite recipe.

Cereal Mix (Puppy Chow)

1/2 cup margarine
1/2 cup peanut butter
1/2 cup peanut butter chips or chocolate chips
1/2 box corn Chex cereal
2 cups powdered sugar

Combine the margarine, peanut butter and chips in a saucepan. Heat until melted. Remove from the heat. Stir in the cereal until well coated. Pour 1 cup powdered sugar into a gallon-size plastic bag. Add the cereal and shake to coat. Add the remaining powdered sugar and shake again. Store in an airtight container.

A fun snack for children and adults that looks like puppy chow.

Peanut Butter Chocolate Kisses

3/4 cup firmly packed brown sugar
1/2 cup chunky peanut butter
1/3 cup butter or margarine
1 egg
1 teaspoon vanilla extract
1 1/3 cups self-rising flour, sifted
40 large milk chocolate kisses

Combine the brown sugar, peanut butter and butter in a mixing bowl; beat until thoroughly blended. Add the egg and vanilla; blend well. Add the flour; blend well. Cover and refrigerate about 1 hour. Shape the dough into 1-inch balls. Place on uncoated baking sheets. Bake at 375 degrees for 5 minutes. Remove baking sheets from the oven. Press a chocolate kiss into the center of each cookie. Return to the oven. Bake 3 minutes; watch carefully to avoid burning chocolate. Transfer the cookies to wire racks to cool. Cool completely before storing.

Makes 40 cookies.

This is Carrie Gabbard's 1989 Madison County 4-H Bake-Off winning recipe.

Betty Overly's Bourbon Balls

1 egg white
4 tablespoons butter (not margarine)
1/2 cup bourbon
Powdered sugar (about 8 cups)
8 ounces semisweet chocolate (tempered*)

Combine the egg white, butter, bourbon and powdered sugar in a large mixing bowl and mix until well blended. Add enough powdered sugar to make a stiff dough. Chill for 3 to 4 hours. Roll into small balls. Dip the balls in the chocolate and place on waxed paper to cool. Place a pecan half on top. Store in tin in a cool place.

*Tempering is a special process of heating and cooling chocolate to specific temperatures to prepare for coating. Tempering chocolate will allow chocolate coatings to stay glossy and firm at room temperature without the addition of wax or paraffin. Paraffin is no longer a FDA approved food additive and is not meant for human consumption. Use commercially made coatings or temper chocolate when using as a coating.

Try this method:

Begin by melting about 2/3 of your chocolate to about 118 degrees in the top of a double boiler. This allows all fat to be melted, but not separate. Transfer the chocolate to a bowl. Gradually add the remaining chocolate, some of it in large lumps to the melted chocolate in the bowl. By adding this new "tempered" chocolate, it will cool and form the desired crystals needed for decorating and coating. Continue stirring in the pieces until it reaches a temperature of about 88 degrees. Remove any remaining chocolate lumps and reuse to temper another batch of chocolate. The chocolate is ready to use at this point. If the chocolate cools to 77 degrees, the tempering process will need to be repeated.

Some say this is time consuming and not worth it. But "chocolate is the spice of life." After tempering a couple of times you will become an expert and develop your own signature products for holidays and special occasions.

Chocolate Hints:

Never heat chocolate over 120 degrees, as it will become unusable.

Small amounts of water may cause the chocolate to "seize," loose its gloss, tighten and be unusable.

Chocolate can be melted by using the microwave or over a pan of water.

Always begin with chocolate pieces no more than 1 inch in size to expedite the process.

Betty Overly, former Bourbon County Extension Agent, is well known throughout Central Kentucky for her holiday delights. There is no telling how many bourbon balls she has made over the years. We always say that Kentucky bourbon is what makes them so good. Maker's Mark and Woodford Reserve are our favorite for these treasures. Betty always stressed the importance of good quality ingredients to make the best product. She would say "don't use the cheap brands, especially on sugar, chocolate and bourbon!"

Heath Bars

40 graham crackers
1/2 cup butter
1/2 cup margarine
1/2 cup sugar
1 cup chopped pecans
6-ounce package chocolate chips

Break the graham crackers into 4 pieces and place on a parchment paper-lined baking sheet. Combine the butter, margarine and sugar in a glass mixing bowl. Microwave on high for 1 minute. Stir and microwave until the mixture boils for 2 minutes. Remove from the microwave and let bubbles die down. Stir and pour the mixture over the crackers. Sprinkle the pecans on top. Bake at 350 degrees for 12 minutes. Melt the chocolate chips and spoon 1/2 teaspoon on top of each graham cracker. Remove and cool on waxed paper.

This is a favorite holiday or special occasion cookie.

Pineapple Cram Pie

3 egg yolks
2/3 cup sugar
1/3 cup flour
1/8 teaspoon salt
1 cup milk
1 cup crushed pineapple
1 tablespoon butter, melted
2 tablespoons lemon juice
1 baked piecrust

Beat the egg yolks in a large bowl. Add the sugar, flour and salt and mix well. Add the milk and pineapple. Transfer to the top of a double boiler and cook until thick and creamy, stirring frequently. Add the butter and lemon juice and mix well. Pour the batter into the piecrust.

Meringue

3 egg whites
5 tablespoons sugar

Beat the egg whites in a medium bowl until stiff. Add the sugar and beat until creamy. Spread the meringue over the filling. Bake for 12 minutes in a moderately slow oven.

This recipe is from James Neale, long time Richmond resident. It is pictured on page 119.

index

Appetizers

Beverages

Breads

Breakfast

Desserts & Sweets

Entrées

Salads

Soups

Tea Sandwiches